The Handbook of Private Practice in Psychology

The Handbook of Private Practice in Psychology

By

EDMUND SHIMBERG, Ph.D.

BRUNNER/MAZEL, Publishers • New York

Library of Congress Cataloging in Publication Data

Shimberg, Edmund, 1925-
    The handbook of private practice in psychology.

    Includes index.
    1. Clinical psychology—Practice.   I.   Title.
RC467.S483   658'.91'1579   79-1518
ISBN 0-87630-197-9

Copyright © 1979 by Edmund Shimberg

Published by
BRUNNER/MAZEL, INC.
19 Union Square
New York, New York 10003

MANUFACTURED IN THE UNITED STATES OF AMERICA

TO

ROBERT D. WEITZ, Ph.D.

teacher

inspiration

friend

Foreword

Private practicing psychologists have a lot of problems in common. They work alone in many cases and have to deal constructively with loneliness. One way of dealing with loneliness constructively is through sharing and exchanging information and experiences in order to learn from one another. This book shares and exchanges information and experiences about issues unique to private practice: (1) how to run an office properly (psychological economics) and in a business-like way; (2) how clinical techniques in private practice differ from clinical techniques in a hospital or clinic (there is no "institutional mother" to absorb the shocks; the psychologist is his own institution—he has total responsibility and he has to absorb the shocks); (3) how the private practitioner is his own "image-maker" in the community—how he becomes the most "grass-roots" of all psychologists when he functions as the agent who provides service to schools, agencies, professionals and private citizens. This kind of "image-making" has its own "bag of tricks" and its own accountability; (4) how new practitioners, uncomfortable in this new role (because our training doesn't include preparation for private practice) can deal with this kind of anxiety constructively.

Anyone in private practice has had a firsthand encounter with anxiety. Anyone contemplating private practice as a vocational vehicle has encountered this anxiety. Accurate information is a good antidote for anxiety. When this information comes from an individual who has actually experienced the "trial-by-fire" anxiety of clinical practice in the private setting and dealt with it constructively with solutions that work, a published account of such an experience is worth reading by both neophytes and veterans. *The Handbook of Private Practice in Psychology* is such an account.

As a private practicing psychologist with over 20 years of experience and as an officer in several professional psychological organizations, Edmund Shimberg is highly qualified to write authoritatively on the subject.

Reading this book puts the pieces of the puzzle together painlessly. The style of the book is as warm and communicative as the style of the man. Most importantly, this book is a capsule of clinical clarity—an invaluable aid as we confront the issues facing us in the ever-expanding world of private practice in psychology. This book can be a teaching tool that can be especially valuable to new Ph.D.'s, new Psy.D.'s and new Ed.D.'s just beginning their professional careers. Those of us who are already established in private practice will also find several worthwhile suggestions for improving our operations in this book.

LEWIS W. FIELD, PH.D.
Clinical and Consulting Psychologist
President, American Society of
Psychologists in Private Practice

Contents

Preface

Three things are necessary
for the salvation of man: to
know what he ought to believe;
to know what he ought to desire;
and to know what he ought to do.

ST. THOMAS AQUINAS, 1273

I began my private practice of psychology many, many years ago with a good number of preconceived ideas and notions as to how to go about it. I discovered, in fairly short order, that most of these ideas were wrong! Since then, increasingly large numbers of psychologists, social workers, marriage counselors, and others in the mental health professions have opted for private practice. Among these are those new to the field as well as more mature professionals with years of agency, hospital, or teaching experience. Most of these colleagues have entered independent practice with the same kind of erroneous preconceptions that I had. Time, it seems, has not been the teacher, after all.

After running some workshops on "The Nuts and Bolts of Private Practice" at conventions, I discovered that there are many mental health professionals hungry for specific and concrete knowledge about the "how to" of independent practice.

Thus, I came to write this book, which is not, incidentally, either a scholarly or theoretical work. It contains no thoughts on the desirability of one theoretical construct vis-à-vis another, and it does not give instructions or directions for psychodiagnosis, the psychotherapeutic management of particular patients, or counseling techniques. Nor, in my view, should it. However, it is the effort of a private practitioner in psychology to share perceptions, based upon trial-and-error experience, about how to enter the independent practice of the mental health professions in the easiest and most efficient manner, and then how to make the practice successful and personally gratifying. Other than those few sections addressed specifically to the psychodiagnostic consultation ("testing," if you will), the book is, I feel, appropriate and useful for any mental health professional wishing to enter independent practice.

Every effort has been made to make the book easily understandable and to answer the questions that most beginning practitioners seem to have. There are few polysyllables and hardly any pontificating.

I hope you find it useful. Good luck in your private practice.

E.S.

Haddonfield, New Jersey
February, 1979

Acknowledgments

This book all started with Murray Benimoff, who so kindly gave me time and a room at the Eastern Psychological Association convention in which to run the first workshop on the nuts and bolts of private practice. Robert Lynch, Vice President of Penn Mutual Insurance Company gave unstintingly of his time and energy to provide information about insurance, professional corporations, and myriad other matters in those areas. Leon Wilson, Esq., counsel to the New Jersey Psychological Association, was most helpful in reviewing the material on Psychologists in relation to the law and lawyers and made useful and significant suggestions and comments. A special note of thanks must be made to Mr. Joseph Gebbia, President of the Histacount Corporation of Melville, New York. He was kind enough to have the forms, cards, and letterheads printed for this book. Patricia Speeks laboriously typed manuscript from my poorly typed and badly corrected originals while, at the same time, providing valuable criticisms of style and spelling.

Most of all, though, my wife/professional associate, Betty, provided the impetus and inspiration for all of this. She provided the structure upon which I have attempted to build the body of this book, and she then read and re-read manuscript —always offering cogent (and some pungent) suggestions. Betty, in her usual self-effacing way, has refused co-authorship and this is my only way of really acknowledging her role in the production of this book.

The Handbook of
Private Practice
in Psychology

1

Is Private Practice for You?

The major assumption of this book is that the reader either has already decided to enter private practice or is seriously contemplating the advisability of so doing. Ordinarily, for this individual, the first questions that come to mind are: "Can I succeed professionally?" "Is there a need for *my* services?" "Can I succeed financially?" Before one can explore the answer to these and other questions, it is necessary to examine the qualifications and requirements necessary to enter practice. These requirements and qualifications have to do with the *individual,* in terms of the kind of professional work he wants to do over and above statutory demand.

One old saw about private practice is, "In private practice the boss works you half to death, but at least you know he has your best interests at heart." And another says, "I'm the only boss I know that I really respect and can really get along with." Hopefully, though, these are not the only reasons for going into private practice. Other psychologists want to go into practice because of the aura, the mystique, the glamour of private practice. (There really isn't any.) Frankly, none of these should be the most compelling reason.

Private practice in psychotherapy is an awesome responsibility, and it requires a great deal of introspection and self-evaluation before the decision to begin a practice is made.

3

The basis, of course, must be the three legs of *training/education, licensure* (or *certification*), and a personal *readiness* for practice.

The private practice of any profession should not be undertaken by anyone who is not fully and adequately trained to assume the responsibility for patients/clients. This is true for the therapist, the psychodiagnostician, the industrial consultant, etc. Training and experience are the only teachers, and they must be adequate to meet the needs of the practice. You are the final decision maker and, in the case of the clinical practice, very often the pivotal person in the lives of the patients you see. Training and education, consequently, must be adequate to permit you to assume this responsibility alone, with no supervisor down the hall and with no department head to pick up the pieces. While there are no precise guidelines set down as yet, at this stage of the development of the profession, a doctorate and some years of experience in the field of choice are the sine qua non. Just how much experience, and of what variety, is still a largely individual matter and must still be left to the discretion and ethical orientation of the practitioner. Clearly, though, one must feel (and be) in a state of readiness before striking off alone.

Licensure and/or certification are required by most states at this time. However, this, alone, is often not enough. The possession of a license indicates that the professional has met the minimal requirements for practice although he may not, in fact, really be ready to go it alone. Have you, for example, had adequate training and supervision in psychodiagnostic evaluations so you can provide consulting services to referral sources without, yourself, needing regular consultation? Have you seen a wide enough variety of therapy patients, under close supervision, so that you can now treat your own cases—alone? Is your experience broad enough so that you know what kinds of patients you can, or cannot, work with? My personal feeling is that few therapists can work successfully with *every* patient that pops up in the office. If you choose to specialize, have you had adequate training in the specialty? Such training should extend beyond a course or two in graduate school or a patient or two during your internship.

Finally, and perhaps most importantly, are you ready—really ready—to go into private practice? Have you looked at all of the ramifications and all of the demands of private practice? There are many. And that's what this chapter is all about.

Private practice is not necessarily for everyone. If you determine that it isn't for you, this doesn't, in any way, mean that you are not a competent psychologist or a worthy person. On the contrary, if, after carefully exploring the issue, you reach the conclusion that it isn't for you, then you have made a meaningful career decision which you should respect. However, if you feel that it *is* for you, then you must be ready to tackle several roles in addition to that of professional psychologist. Some of these roles are: office manager, director, policy setter, bill collector, public relations person, businessperson, and, finally, Jack (Jane)-of-all-trades.

Offering private care services to the community implies a readiness and desire to set the highest possible standards for oneself. It demands the most ethical procedures and the most efficient possible functioning. The people who come to see you are placing themselves in your hands, and they are entitled to nothing short of the best. Your professional career depends on your expertise, since there are a number of other places for your patients to turn if you don't do an adequate job of helping them. President Harry S. Truman had a sign on his desk in the Oval Office which read, "The Buck Stops Here." So it is in private practice—the buck, indeed, stops here.

As you consider setting up your own practice, you should ask if your present successes with patients are based upon the good supervision you are receiving, or the supportive structure of your work environment. Or are you really going it alone within (or despite) your present milieu? Remember, your reputation (translate that to mean "success") in private practice is what determines how well you eat! Further, you should consider that, in addition to the demands of professional functioning, there is a myriad of questions which arise in the everyday functioning of your office! "When do I order the new stationery?" "Do I need a new supply of toilet paper in the john?" "The waiting room carpet is wearing thin. Shall I replace it now or wait another six months?" "How do I set realistic fees—and collect them?" "How come I haven't received any new referrals in the past three weeks?" "I haven't gotten a referral from Dr. Jones in a long time. Did I mess up that last case he sent me?" "Do I pay my bills and take the rest home? Or, shall I budget myself and draw a set amount each week?"

Are you prepared to sit down at the typewriter and prepare your own reports to referral sources? Is your spouse ready and able to do this? If so, for how long? Shall you hire a typist/receptionist and how much do you pay her? The list of questions goes on and on.

Many professionals in private practice speak of the loneliness they feel. They talk of being in the office day after day with no one to talk to, other than patients. Well, private practice can, indeed, be lonely—if one makes it lonely. However, there are others who, instead, feel that they are there by choice, and that going it alone is the way that they function best. Private practice provides them with maximum personal and professional gratification. These colleagues do not see it as "loneliness"; they see it as doing the work they choose in the way they have chosen.

For the individual who wants to practice independently, but who also needs colleague contact and stimulation, there are viable alternatives to the full-time, one-person practice. One can, for example, organize or join a group practice. There can be a partnership practice, or one can rent space from a colleague. Some people choose to be in an essentially full-time, independent practice but spend some hours a week in a part-time or consulting capacity in order to receive the stimulation and feedback that they need from colleagues.

More and more private practitioners are joining, or organizing, groups for continuing education. This is a splendid way to learn, to keep current, and to form relationships with others in the field. It is also a way to develop possible sources of referral. Additionally, continuing education is receiving increasing impetus from licensing bodies and state Psychological Associations and will, no doubt, become a necessary requirement for maintenance of licensure before very much longer. There are also all kinds of continuing education programs held throughout the year by groups organized for that purpose. So, whatever your own, individual needs may be in terms of "otherness," there is a way to meet and satisfy these needs in private practice.

Another frequently raised question has to do with vacations. In private practice, after all, there is no agency or hospital that grants paid time off. You are the agency, and you are the administrator. The private practitioner does make vacation time available and, in fact, must! One of the most difficult things for the beginning private practitioner to do is to simply take time off for self. Ordinarily, the tendency is to try to work as many days a week as possible because of the anxiety attendant upon depending totally upon oneself for sustenance. Don't do it. Vacations must be taken, and the practice will not suffer. If you don't take time off, you will suffer and so will the practice.

In some kinds of group practice there is provision for continuing income while a member of the group is stretched out on the warm sands of a far off beach or is at the tiller of his sailboat. If you choose to incorporate your practice (see Chapter 2), you can also "build in" vacation provisions.

Still another question has to do with "sick leave." In the individual practice there isn't any provision for illness, unless, again, it is built into your corporation. Also, in a group practice there may be specific provisions made for a sick-leave-with-pay arrangement for members of the group.

As you set up your private practice you should become familiar with major medical insurance policies which will cover most of the expenses of catastrophic illness, as well as income protection plans which will provide ongoing monies while the policyholder is laid up over a long period of time. Both of these coverages are available through the American Psychological Association and some major insurance companies.

Unlike practitioners in most agency or hospital settings, private practitioners do not have an automatic retirement program. Therefore, you are also going to be responsible for planning for your own future in terms of setting both long- and short-term goals. Many people stay in institutional settings because of this factor—they need the security of a retirement program. In fact, though, the private practitioner can have a retirement program which is superior to one provided in an institutional setting while, at the same time, providing tax benefits (see Chapter 9).

It would seem that for every "negative" there is a corresponding possible "positive." In fact, the major determinant in choosing private practice as a career choice is the desire to do it. If it is what you really want, the obstacles will seem small when compared to the overall rewards. What, then, are some of the rewards? The first, or at least the one that should be uppermost in one's mind, is the opportunity to work with other people in a helping profession. And, hand in hand with this is the opportunity to do precisely what you want to do in the way you want to do it. It is *only* in private practice that one has the chance to utilize the skills, talent, and training that have been developed over the years in ways that are completely satisfying to oneself. It is only in private practice that one can assume the full and total responsibility for the delivery of professional services and deliver these services in ways that are not externally determined. What you can do and how well you do it are the major determinants. There are no free rides and there is neither contract nor tenure. You stand, or fall, on your own merit.

It is only in private practice that one can decide what kinds of cases to see and what kinds of approaches to utilize. There are no clinic policies to which one must adhere and the length of time you see a patient is determined by you. You work (or overwork) the number of hours you choose. The private practitioner may well be among the most fortunate of humans, for who else can really claim to be doing the kind of work he chooses, with the people he chooses to work with?

And, finally, there are the financial rewards of private practice. In the final analysis, your income will be limited only by the number of hours per week you choose to work. A properly organized and managed practice is bound to be successful. And that's what this book is all about.

2
Kinds of Practice

Most people entering private practice think of it as being basically a one-person affair and, most of the time, it is. However, there are variations on the theme which are being increasingly played. In partnership or group practices the methodology of establishing and running the practice remains essentially the same as for the solo practice except that when more than one person is involved the possible complications increase in a geometric, rather than arithmetic, way. In this chapter I will sort out some of the pieces of the various kinds of practice without, however, covering legal aspects of such arrangements.

PARTNERSHIP PRACTICE

There are two basic kinds of partnership practices, each of which has subdivisions. The first kind might also be called an associative practice. That is, two practitioners decide that they will share office space and that is all. Each furnishes his own office, and they share the expense of furnishing the waiting room, maintaining toilet facilities, and paying for cleaning service. Each has his own letterhead, telephone service, and all the other accoutrements of office furnishing mentioned elsewhere in this book. Each obtains his own referrals and manages his own cases. They are in no way otherwise associated other than in the space sharing arrangement, and the fees that each collects are his own, exclusively.

In this instance, the two practitioners must be quite clear about their financial responsibilities—how much, or what percentage, of the operating costs of the office shall each assume? While a handshake or verbal agreement may work fine, it is usually best to consult an attorney and have him draw up an agreement that will be signed by both and be binding on each. With such a carefully drawn agreement there can be little or no ambiguity in the relationship. A written agreement should contain provisions for such possibilities as one of the signatories deciding to move out of the shared space. Who, for example, is then responsible for rent and other expenses? And, for that matter, who signs the original lease? One, the other, or both? What if one of the two people involved also wants to sublet his half of the space to a part-time practitioner? What kind of controls does the other have over this? These, and other possible questions or conflicts can best be resolved, *in advance,* by sitting down with an attorney, allowing him to explore all such areas with you, and then drawing up a mutually agreeable contract. In fact, it might even be best for each of the two professionals concerned to have his own attorney so that there is no possible later question of conflict of interest. In this way, there is no question as to responsibility, and there can be no later, "But I thought we had agreed. . . ."

A variation, which is somewhere between an associative practice and a full partnership practice, is one where there is a primary practitioner who takes an associate or "partial" partner. In such an arrangement, for example, the practitioner assumes total responsibility for the financial aspects of maintaining the office. The associate, on the other hand, has no responsibility of this kind, but merely uses the office space for his work with patients. In this kind of practice the primary practitioner ordinarily refers cases to the associate as they come in to the office. Also, the usual agreement is that the associate consider all referrals made individually to him as being referrals to "the practice." In this way there is minimal confusion over what belongs to whom and how billing shall be accomplished. In other words, the same financial arrangement obtains whether the associate receives referrals directly from the primary practitioner or via his own sources of referral.

In this practice the primary practitioner will ordinarily do all the billing and bookkeeping, and the letterhead and billhead will have both names. The associate will receive a percentage of the fees he collects (usually 60-70%), with the remainder reverting to the primary practitioner for administrative expenses involved in maintaining the office. Thus, this is a special kind of partnership new practitioners often find attractive because it provides them with an entree to practice with none of the expenses involved in setting up an office. It also frequently leads to a full partnership with the primary practitioner. Here, again, the terms of agreement should be quite clear and should be drawn up with the consultation of an attorney.

The final kind of partnership arrangement is the one that could simply be called "full partnership." In such an arrangement, the partners are clearly defined as such. They share mutual letterhead, billhead, telephone listings, etc. They also share fully in the operating costs of the office. In addition, they usually "share" the referrals. That is, unless a prospective patient, for example, specifically requests one of the partners, new cases would be assigned to whichever practitioner is available at the time the referral is received. Monies received in such an arrangement ordinarily go into a common "pool" and, after expenses, are equally shared by the partners.

Such an arrangement takes an extraordinary amount of trust on the part of each partner, along with very clear understanding as to the responsibilities of each, in terms of hours to be worked, speaking engagements to be undertaken, etc. Again, the contract between the two (or more) must be clear and totally unambiguous. Partnerships such as this can be an excellent arrangement in terms of one partner "covering" cases for the other at vacation times, sharing cases in terms of conjoint family therapy, or when one sees child and the other sees parent, etc.

Any partnership arrangement, be it an associate relationship or one involving full partnership, is very much like a marriage. The partners must be really compatible, should complement each other in terms of disposition, personality characteristics, and, in the professional sense, technical skills and orientation. That is not to say that each must be identical in all of these features but, rather, each should provide a balance for the other in the overall relationship. Further, despite the appropriate precautions of legal documentation that must be undertaken, there must be a great amount of trust and respect between the partners. Indeed, as in any marriage, the possibility of divorce is always there. And, at times, the divorce can be destructive to both partners.

EMPLOYER/EMPLOYEE

In addition to the foregoing kinds of professional relationships, there can be an actual employer/employee relationship. In such a case an established psychologist employs a colleague to work with him in the practice and pays him on a mutually agreed upon basis. The employer has all of the usual responsibilities toward the employed psychologist that obtain in any such relationship.

Ordinarily, when a psychologist enters a practice as an

employee it is with the understanding that there will be the opportunity for a partnership arrangement if the relationship works out well for both. This, too, can be a good way for a beginning practitioner to get his feet wet in practice and see if it meets his needs for a viable professional life-style.

GROUP PRACTICE

The group practice is very much like the partnership arrangement, except that there are usually more than two members of the group and each of the members ordinarily brings special skills to the group. For example, one may specialize in therapy with children and adolescents, another may possess special expertise in psychodiagnostics, while a third might be primarily interested in behavior modification. Additionally, group practices frequently have, as members of the group, psychiatric social workers, educational specialists, speech or reading therapists, etc. Thus, the group practice can be one that functions like a private community mental health facility.

The advantages to such a practice lie in the fact that it can provide a broad spectrum service to the community and that each of the professionals involved has immediate access to colleagues who can provide ancillary services for his patients. Additionally, it is an excellent way of avoiding the loneliness associated with private practice. A group practice also provides the greatest opportunities for the provision of "benefits" like paid vacations, sick leave, retirement benefits, etc. In such a practice the members of the group usually draw a salary based upon the numbers of patient contact hours they work per week. There is usually a profit-sharing arrangement at the end of each fiscal year, at which time additional monies are divided, again according to the actual work performed by each member of the group.

FORMING A CORPORATION

This section on professional corporations should probably most properly appear in the chapter dealing with planning for the future. However, since we are here talking about the various kinds of practice, corporate practice is included for the sake of homogeneity.

The formation of corporations is a relatively recent development for professionals in practice. As a result, there is probably more mystery, confusion, and misinformation about this aspect of practice than almost any other.

First, let's define. A professional corporation is a *tax-saving* technique that was designed for high-income professionals in order to provide them with the employee benefits available to commercial business corporations. Some of these tax-deductible benefits include pension and profit-sharing plans, group term life insurance, medical insurance, automobile expenses, home office expense allowances, and other so-called fringe benefits available to corporations.

Next, what are the usual criteria one should consider before giving serious thought to incorporation? There are four general characteristics of the practitioner that must be considered: (1) *Net income*—the general criterion for incorporating a professional ordinarily requires that the net income be in the range of $45,000 to $65,000. Gross income is irrelevant because the key factor is the net taxable income from the practice. Ordinarily, if a practitioner is making less than $45,000, it generally would not pay him to consider incorporation. However, there are exceptions, such as the single professional, who arrives at the 50 percent tax bracket much earlier than the married person. (2) *The ability to save*—incorporation is for the practitioner who is already saving $5,000 to $10,000 a year which is not being used for discretionary spending. This can be in many forms, such as a contribution to a Keogh or HR-10 plan, premiums for life insurance, mutual funds, saving plans, or anything else that is not being used for current spending. If, on the other hand, the practitioner is spending every cent that is being made, then incorporation is not indicated—no matter how much he is earning. (3) *Family life-style*—here, one must look at such things as current spending habits and the need for accumulating monies to purchase or decorate a house, educate children in private schools or colleges, pay for weddings or other family affairs, repay debts, and so on. If an individual is heavily burdened by these items, second thoughts should be given to incorporation. (4) *A general philosophical acceptance of the discipline of a corporation*—this is not a problem for most individuals, but it is something that must be considered. Unless the practitioner can be shown by his financial advisors how to properly maintain records and everything else that goes with the professional corporation, then that corporation is both doomed to failure and possible problems with the Internal Revenue Service.

In every state of the U.S. an individual may incorporate as a solo professional; there is no prohibition of any kind. A group of professionals may do the same. In fact, in a group practice of three or four psychologists, for example, one might want to incorporate. He then incorporates by himself and his corporation becomes a member of the group.

Having met the basic criteria, the best way to begin a corporation is to first have a meeting with your accountant and any other advisors in order to consider the feasibility, cost, and savings of a corporation. In this way you will be able to make an intelligent decision as to whether to consider this option. Once that decision is made, the mechanics are to file articles of incorporation with the state corporation bureau and to follow through with all of the other details of incorporating. These include determining the proper by-laws, minutes of meetings, employment contracts and shareholders agreements, and establishing a medical reimbursement plan, a salary and expense allowance program, and a retirement plan. All these items can usually be handled within a six-to-eight-week period.

If you do decide to incorporate, you may anticipate a tax savings of approximately $2,000 to $5,000 per year, providing you have met the criteria outlined previously. This is not, of course, a hard and fast statement but is, rather, based upon the experiences of many who have already incorporated.

There are some practitioners who wonder at the effect of incorporation upon professional autonomy. In fact, it has no effect whatsoever. If you are in a group, you still have all the advantages and disadvantages of the group in making decisions. If you are a solo practitioner, the fact that you have incorporated has no effect on your decision-making capability. Insofar as the community is concerned, the only difference the public ever sees are the initials "P.C." (Professional Corporation), "P.A." (Professional Association), or Ltd. after your name.

The major impact on you will be in the financial sense. Along with the benefits of tax savings and retirement planning, you will have to accept the discipline of a salary paid to you by the corporation (although *you* will determine that salary) and records to maintain.

The corporate structure, with all of its advantages, may not necessarily be indicated for the more senior practitioner who feels that it is too constricting for his professional lifestyle in terms of personal management of finances. In other words, there are many professionals who feel most comfortable with the ABC technique of practice: A—how much did I make last month? B—how much is left after expenses? C—take home B.

3

Setting Up the Office

Now you have made the decision to go into practice. What comes first? Well, ordinarily one should decide *where* to practice. This is an extremely important decision which can affect the direction your practice will take. For example, shall you practice at home and set a room aside for that purpose? Do you want to see patients in the setting where you are employed? Will you share space with a colleague or another professional of a different discipline? Shall you rent a regular office of your own, and where? Is it better to buy your own building? Let's look at all of these situations, since each has its own merits and negative features.

THE OFFICE AT HOME

Many psychologists find it most convenient and financially feasible to simply set aside space in their own home or apartment for their practice. It means having a place which is only for the office and furnished as such. The home office should, if possible, be separated from the rest of the house. You will need quiet, without any of the usual family noises filtering through. In order for this office to be eligible for the tax benefits of a business deduction, you will need a separate entrance, and you will have to be able to convince the Internal

18

Revenue Service that it is used exclusively for your practice. There are two main advantages to the home office: It is convenient and it requires no additional expense for rent or mortgage payments. Your basic expenditures will be for furnishings and possibly for some structural modification.

However, there are disadvantages to working at home. If you work in the evening, as many practitioners do, your family may have to tiptoe around so they don't disturb you and your patients. If you see children as patients, you may encounter resentment from your *own* children: "How come you play with strange kids and not with me?" And your patients will learn a great deal about you in terms of your family and lifestyle. If it is important to you, in terms of your theoretical orientation or personal needs, to allow your patients to know only minimal facts about your personal life, then consider carefully before beginning your practice at home.

Before setting up an office at home you should consult your local zoning board. Your community may have restrictions concerning businesses and professional offices at home, requiring a zoning variance. If you live in a small community, what are the attitudes about the mental health professions? Will prospective patients have concerns about being seen going into your office in your neighborhood? What are the attitudes of your neighbors about you, your practice, and "the kinds of people" you will be seeing? Will they resent cars parked in the neighborhood? If you don't have a waiting room, how will they feel about strangers sitting in those parked cars for long periods of time? (Remember, if you see children, the parent(s) have to wait somewhere!) Also, not having a waiting room may mean spacing your appointments at greater intervals which is costly of your time and, hence, can limit your income.

You may want to consider the availability of public transportation. If there is none available, your practice will be automatically limited to car driving adults. Adolescents, for example, whose independence you may want to encourage, will not be able to get to your office alone. If you have a family, can they tolerate having you around all day, drifting in for a cup of coffee when you have a cancellation or an open appointment? On the other hand, of course, when you work at home you do not have to contend with driving, traffic hassles, tolls, and getting to the office in bad weather. Also, the free time thus made available can be used for writing, research, and study.

THE OFFICE-AT-THE-OFFICE

Many of those beginning in private practice decide to practice part-time, using the facilities of the setting of their primary employment. This immediately cuts overhead expenses to zero (or close to it). There are other benefits, as well. The office-at-the-office removes all the pressure of an initial financial investment for furnishings. It may well provide a baseline of referral sources when your colleagues learn that you are now available to see private patients as well. There can be a great deal of comfort in knowing that there is someone down the hall with whom you can have a quick "corridor consultation" about a problem case or diagnostic question. And, like the office at home, it is convenient.

At the same time, though, you should carefully explore the policy of the setting in which you work. Will they permit you to conduct a private practice there and, if so, what are the rules? Can you see anyone you choose? Will you be limited to only a certain number of hours per week? Can you come in, for your own practice, at times when the office is ordinarily closed? Some settings place a limit on the amount of outside income you can make, and some have a fee sharing policy where a portion of your fees must revert to the agency. Find out if you can have letterhead and billhead printed, using the address of the agency (and their telephone number), and how they feel about private patients calling. If you see your private patients during the regular working day, make friends with the secretary/receptionist. She'll want to know who is a private patient and who belongs to the agency so that billing doesn't become a problem. Also, you don't want to incur her wrath for making extra, confusing work because she has to sort out patients for you.

Finally, practicing at the office may present a problem of identity for the practitioner. The identification with the agency itself may inhibit others' perception of you as a private practitioner. This, in turn, could limit the number of referrals you could receive. In other words, you may be seen as a some-time practitioner or as someone who is not really committed to practice. On the other hand, the office-at-the-office could be a good way to get your feet wet and decide if private practice is really for you. If a limited, very part-time involvement is what you want—fine! This could be it. If, after trying it for awhile, you decide that private practice simply isn't your cup of tea, then you can extricate yourself with no major loss of investment. And if this experience is a positive one for you, then you may opt for greater involvement in terms of establishing an office away from the office.

SHARING OFFICE SPACE

Renting or sharing space with another professional is yet another way of setting up practice. Psychologists share space with pediatricians, internists, attorneys, dentists, CPA's, realtors, and any number of other kinds of professionals, including other psychologists. Again, it is a fine way to eliminate some of the expenses involved in setting up an office on your own. Most often such space is rented (shared) from a professional who is already in practice and either has more space than can be utilized or is known personally to the psychologist and wants to help him get started. The classified advertisement section of your local newspaper is a good source of potential shared rental space. When making such an arrangement, explore with the prime rentor whether or not you can hang out a shingle, send out announcements using that address, and whether or not you can either have your own telephone or have your name used when his is answered.

Obviously, one of the negative features of such an arrangement is the possibility of, as in the office-at-the-office, losing or never establishing your own unique public identity as a private practitioner. You must also consider how well you can get along with the prime rentor. Can you live in close proximity to him day after day? Very often, in the shared arrangement, you will simply have to "make do" with the space available. This may mean an office that is not furnished to your tastes, or inadequate storage space, or any of a host of possible minor inconveniences.

RENTING AN OFFICE OF YOUR OWN

This, certainly, is one of the two ways of practicing that most clearly and unquestionably identifies you as a private practitioner—one who is fully committed to practice and "here to stay." Renting an office doesn't necessarily mean that you are committed to a full-time endeavor all at once. Many psychologists rent their own office and use it for a part-time practice permanently, or until they are ready to make the change to a full-time commitment.

In renting an office, the two major decisions to be made are (a) where you want to locate, and (b) how much you want to pay in rent. Most office buildings charge rental based on square feet of space rented on a per annum basis. Thus, if you need 900 square feet and rent is $8.00 per square foot, you will pay $7200 per year, or $600.00 per month. Offices in converted private homes ordinarily rent at a flat monthly fee, and the rental is usually based upon the factors of desirability of location and the use to which it is put, i.e., offices requiring extensive renovation usually rent for more.

When seeking out your own individual office to rent, there are certain things to look for: Is there parking in a lot, or is adequate on-the-street parking available? Are you close to public transportation? If there are other tenants in the building, is their business or practice the kind with which you want to be identified? (You may not want to be in the same building with a practicing Druid or a fortune teller.)

In considering the neighborhood in which you want to practice, there are three generic choices: "doctor's row"; a quiet residential neighborhood with few, if any, other professional offices; or an impersonal office building with both professional and non-professional offices in it. Also to be considered in the "quiet residential neighborhood" category are those apartment buildings, usually found in large cities, that have professional office space off the entrance lobby. Ordinarily these spaces are specifically designed for professional office utilization and meet all of the usual criteria for office rental. Most of the time they are at ground level and, depending on the big city where you practice, may require special security. That is, you should be sure that windows are safe from entry and that the lobby itself is secure. If there is a doorman, you should ask if he is on duty 24 hours a day and if all visitors are screened. If this is the case, you must consider how your patients will feel about identifying themselves as your patients and, in fact, what are the doorman's attitudes towards people going to a "shrink." It could be helpful to speak to the doorman, after you have begun to move in, and orient him towards you, your patients, and the fact that they (and he) might be anxious, etc. Other than these special considerations, the apartment building rental is no different from any other. Each type of location has both positives and negatives, and you must decide which one will best meet your needs in terms of the type of practice you want to develop, the "flavor" of the community in which you will practice, and your own personal needs, wishes, and predelictions. Further, you should consider if the office space will meet your needs not only now, but also for the foreseeable future.

When you decide on a rental office, get all the terms in writing! A lease, even a month-to-month lease, should be in writing, and should spell out all of your obligations and, perhaps even more important, should spell out all of the landlord's obligations. Who provides heat? Electricity? Hot water? May you freely renovate, if you wish, or will this cause a rental increase? Must you obtain the landlord's permission to install window air conditioners? Very often it is most desirable to consult an attorney and have him read the lease (after all, the lease is written in *his* professional jargon, not ours). The small fee he will charge can save you many potential headaches in the long run.

BUYING YOUR OWN BUILDING

Buying a building of your own is a lot easier than you may think, and has many advantages. First, it is *yours,* to do with as you wish. You can remodel it in any way you choose, and you can take as long to do it as you wish. All the expenses of renovation are deductible, in various ways, as business expenses and so the actual cost to you is decreased accordingly (that is, money that would have been paid as income tax is now used for improving your property).

Buying a property that will be used only for your offices is not the best idea unless, of course, you are a very private person. Most professionals buy an income-producing property which serves as their own office and also has other space available for rental either as office space to other professionals or as apartments. Either way, the net result of having your own building is to sharply reduce your monthly operating costs while at the same time giving you ample office space and a property that will increase in value over the years.

On the other hand, you must decide if you want to be a landlord. Being the Lord of the Manor may involve tenant problems from time to time. You may, for example, find that you have rented an apartment to someone who proves to be undesirable. (It can be very disconcerting to you and your patients to have a shrieking parent overhead day after day.)

Further, as the landlord you are responsible for the leaky faucets, broken furnace, and cracked driveway. However, there is a way out! Most reputable realtors will be glad to act as manager of the property for a small fee, based upon monthly rental. That is, they will collect the rent for you and receive a percentage of it. For this fee, they will handle all the problems that may arise. While you are responsible for ultimate payment for repairs and maintenance, the realtor does all the dirty work of getting the plumber, electrician, etc. Your realtor will also handle the actual rental for you—advertising the rental and screening potential tenants.

Purchasing your own building is probably much easier than you have thought. Lending institutions are usually delighted to lend money to professional people, and they will go out of their way to help. If you have the cash available for a down payment and want to use your savings for this purpose, then you are well on your way. If you don't have the cash, or if you don't want to use what cash you have as a down payment, there are still other ways to enter into property ownership. One of them is to use your present home, if you have one, as the basis for obtaining a second mortgage, the proceeds of which are then used for the down payment on your office property. This sounds complicated, but a reliable realtor can be of great help in making all the arrangements.

If you have made the decision to buy, what must you look for? The considerations are just about the same as for the previously discussed arrangements except that even more care in selection is needed. After all, you are buying this place and intend to use it for a long time, so it is important that it is exactly what you want for now and that it will serve in the future when your practice has grown to the point you are hoping it will.

One final word about buying your own building: Consult your attorney about legal ownership of the building. That is, in whose name(s) should it be? Yours alone? Your wife's? Both? You and your partner(s)? This is most important in terms of long-term estate planning. In the case of partnership or group practice, it is critical that the ownership terms be clearly stated in the event of the demise of one of the members or the dissolution of the partnership.

Finally, it is sometimes possible and desirable to buy the practice of a senior practitioner who is retiring or leaving the area. In such an instance you are, in effect, buying an old established firm with all of the positives that may accrue to such an arrangement. More details of this kind of arrangement appear in Chapter 9. However, for our purposes here, suffice it to say that when buying an established practice there are some general rules of thumb by which you should guide your decision. First, is the practice, indeed, a "going concern"? For example, have the books for the past few years been made available to you and your accountant and are they in order? Secondly, have you carefully checked and evaluated the reputation of the practitioner from whom you are making this purchase? Is this the kind of professional with whom you want your name associated for the short time it will be (until you establish your own unique identity in the community)?

And, lastly, does the practice meet all of your criteria in terms of your own needs and plans for the kind of practice you want? If you can answer in the affirmative to all of the foregoing, then you may well be ready to purchase an established practice.

FINDING OFFICE SPACE

Whether you decide to rent or buy, there are a number of ways that you can find the kind of office space you want. One good method is to ask colleagues already in practice if they know of any available office space in their area. They may well know of a vacant office, or building, down the street. A drawback to this is that you may encounter resistance from those who would experience anxiety at the presence of another, similar practitioner in their immediate area.

The classified columns of your local newspaper are often a good source of rental space, except that sometimes one finds that an office described in glowing terms turns out to be, well . . . something less than that described in print. So, if this is the course you choose, you must be prepared to do a lot of legwork.

The classified ads appearing in professional society newsletters are usually accurate and, because of where they have been placed, frequently reflect the needs of a professional looking for office space. Thus, they can be helpful.

Finally, whether you rent or buy, realtors can be enormously helpful. They will do all of your preliminary screening for you. Once you give a reasonably good description of the kind of office or property you want and indicate the general location you desire, as well as how much you can afford, the realtor will try hard to meet your needs.

4

Furnishing the Office

All too many professionals in the mental health area feel that the furnishing of their office is unimportant—that their personal presence and approach to the client are all important. In theory—fine. In practice—not so. Packaging, in our society, is extremely important. Your office—the "package," if you will—is extremely important. The waiting room, for example, is the patient's first introduction to you—and this introduction takes place even before the patient meets you. Thus, the waiting room should be warm, inviting, and carefully calculated to help assuage some of the anxiety that all patients feel on initial contact with a helping professional. It should also be a place where families that are waiting for their child, for example, can be comfortable while you are having your session with the young patient.

Your office should be equally comfortable. This is the place where you will be spending most of your waking hours. You have a right to be comfortable in a setting that meets your own needs for a feeling of ease. Also, the comfort that you feel will be communicated to your patients. The office, in other words, is a special kind of milieu which, in and of itself, conveys a message to patients which can facilitate the work you are trying to do.

28

What kind of space, then, is needed for a new office? The basic requirements are:

(1) waiting room,
(2) your own office,
(3) storage space,
(4) bathroom facilities.

Depending on the kind of practice you are going into, or anticipate having, you may also want to consider:

(5) combination play/diagnostic room,
(6) family/group therapy room,
(7) secretarial space.

WAITING ROOM

The general flavor of the waiting room has already been discussed. Seating arrangements in the waiting room are also very important. If your practice is to be exclusively with adolescents and/or adults, individual seats are most desirable. Most adults coming to a psychologist's office prefer individual seats to couches. On the other hand, if your practice includes children, then a combination of both multiple and single seats are most desirable. Children frequently prefer to sit with the parent who has brought them to the office, and parents frequently have to bring siblings along. Here, again, the siblings usually prefer to sit with the parent.

The style in which you furnish is, of course, a matter of personal taste and preference. But there are some general rules which can be helpful. If your practice is exclusively adolescents and adults, you may, by and large, use almost any kind of waiting room furniture with either fabric or plastic/leather materials. However, if you see children, serviceability becomes very important. Plastic/leather materials stand up to the wear that children can give them and are very easily cleaned. A little soap and water will remove all signs of the sticky candy bar, soiled diaper, or muddy footprints. Also, if you see children, avoid swivel chairs like the plague! Kids love to spin in these, using their heels on your nice, new walls to accelerate their RPM's. The choice of wall coverings, too, is important if you see children. Paint is not the best choice, since handprints have a way of appearing, and after a time, the constant cleaning of them will wear that section of the wall down to the bare plaster or wallboard. A strong, washable wallpaper will last much longer. Wood paneling is often ideal; it is sturdy, easily cleaned, and looks extremely good. Since there is sufficient variety of paneling now available, you can easily find a style that will complement the decor of your waiting room.

The waiting room should have a supply of reading materials that are appropriate for the age groups you see. Try to avoid periodicals that have very long articles and stories; we all find it annoying to be called into the doctor's office when we are in the middle of a fascinating magazine article! News and picture magazines are ordinarily best, with the old reliable *Reader's Digest* probably heading the list of good waiting room reading materials. Children are always delighted to find a supply of comic books and are not at all reluctant to remind you when you should get new ones. In other words, unless you have an extraordinarily erudite patient population, don't try to impress them with your own sophistication or special interests.

The waiting room should also have some facility for hanging coats. If no closet is available, then a coat rack will do fine. If you see children, make certain the coat rack is sturdy and hard to move! And, of course, there should be adequate provision for boots, umbrellas, and other rainwear. If you have a vestibule, this is a good place for a bright little sign (you can have them made of plastic, at your local stationers)

that says, "Please leave boots, overshoes, and umbrellas here."
Then, have a rubber or plastic boot tray and an umbrella
stand right under the sign. If you have no vestibule, put the
sign and the equipment in a corner of the waiting room close
to the door where they can be readily seen. Or, you can
watch your nice new carpet gradually change color all winter
as the wet boots tramp and the umbrellas drip.

It is obvious, by now, that much emphasis has been placed
on the rather special, long-wearing arrangements needed for
the practice in which children are seen. The reason is simple.
First, kids are, indeed, harder on furnishings than are most
adults. However, and perhaps even more importantly, don't
count on parents to do your housekeeping for you. While it is
not the purpose of this book to go into family dynamics, it is
the experience of most child-oriented practitioners that parents frequently give little or no supervision to their children
while in the waiting room and it is not at all unusual to find,
after such a family leaves, that the waiting room looks as
though it was directly in the path of Attila and his Mongol
horde.

Finally, some kind of arrangement for music in the waiting room is important. It is pleasant to listen to while waiting
and serves a secondary function of helping with soundproof-
ing. If possible, have only a loudspeaker in the waiting room,
with the primary radio or stereo system elsewhere. This will
foil the dial twirlers and cut down on the shock of coming
into the waiting room and being blasted with high decibel
hard rock instead of the low decibel Bach you have selected
earlier.

Lamps are far better than overhead lighting in setting a
comfortable, inviting tone in the waiting room. The soft
glow of the lamps will also tend to assuage the anxiety of
the initial visit.

Ashtrays and smoking are a very individual decision. If you

don't wish smoking in your office, a discrete sign and the total absence of ashtrays will get the message across. If you don't mind smoking, then be certain that you use large, strong receptacles for ashes, butts, and the inevitable candy wrappers. Also, if you don't use ashtrays, a wastepaper basket for those candy wrappers, discarded appointment cards, and odds and ends from purses is essential. Waiting rooms, for some reason, seem to be the location of choice for cleaning out wallets and purses of old raffle tickets and last year's calendar.

YOUR OWN OFFICE

Your own office should be, as indicated earlier, clearly a place in which you are comfortable and which is a reflection of you. Except for those therapists who seek (usually unsuccessfully) extreme anonymity from their patients, most practitioners find that a comfortable setting filled with pieces of art and souvenirs which have personal meaning for them add to, rather than detract from, effective work with patients. Basic furnishings should, of course, consist of comfortable seating and a place, ordinarily a desk, for you to work. Here, again, there are a wide range of possibilities for furnishings. Desks may range from a very expensive antique all the way to a stained hollow door set up on a pair of two-drawer file cabinets.

Obviously, you must be comfortable in your office, since you will spend a great deal of time there. But what about your patients? Of course, they must be comfortable as well. It is usually helpful to have a choice of seating for them. Many practitioners find that a deep, comfortable chair, along with a relatively firm, hardbacked seat, will give patients the options they need. Which seat they initially select, incidentally, may also provide you with some clinical cues/clues. Also, if you plan on seeing families, couples, or small groups you should have adequate seating for them. And, of course, if you use a couch in your therapeutic approach, it should be one that is appropriate—an "analytic couch," not a living room model.

STORAGE SPACE

Storage space can range from a closet to a spacious store-room. You must have provisions for locked files holding case materials, shelving for diagnostic materials, stationery, and all the myriad things that have a way of simply accumulating over the years. If you have the space, a small refrigerator can be a boon. It's good for the cool drink you may want in the summer, holds your brown bag lunch on those days you find yourself doing "seat work" during the noon hour, and is great for the perishable kinds of snacks that child therapists often keep for the youngsters. The storage area may be used for office cleaning equipment and supplies, and may well become a repository for old journals.

A couple of easily assembled steel shelving units, which are sturdy and long lasting, will ordinarily serve to store almost anything you may have.

BATHROOM FACILITIES

A bathroom is a bathroom is a bathroom. But there are some items that *your* office john needs. A paper towel dispenser is the most practical way of providing toweling, and wall mounted units are neat, reasonably attractive, and easy to install. Your local janitorial supply house can provide you with the dispenser and will be glad to deliver towels to you. Cakes of soap tend to get messy, dirty, and unappealing. Since many people object to using soap that others have used, an over-the-sink liquid soap dispenser is desirable. Again, your janitorial supply people can provide both dispenser and soap. (Mild liquid dish detergent works equally well and is less expensive.) A wall mounted paper cup dispenser will take care of those cool drinks of water on hot summer days. A large, visible wastepaper basket will handle the used paper towels and cups.

You may want to keep a box of tissues in the washroom as a courtesy and convenience for your patients. However, a box of tissues in your desk drawer is very important. Patients sometimes cry and you may want to blow your nose or clean your spectacles from time to time.

Of course, if you rent space in an office building where the bathroom is down the hall, all you can do is give your patients the key to the executive washroom and hope for the best.

COMBINATION PLAY/DIAGNOSTIC ROOM

The combination play/diagnostic room, if you have one, can be the most Spartan room in your office. It requires a good sized, sturdy table, at least two chairs for seating at the table, and, if possible, a closet or cabinet with adequate shelving for diagnostic and play materials. This closet should be provided with a door. Open closets, filled with play materials, are very distracting (and tempting) to children being seen for diagnostic studies.

The walls and floor should be covered in a sturdy, washable material for the same reasons described in the section on the waiting room. If treatment with children is planned, it can be helpful to have running water in the room. A sink is useful when working with paints and makes cleanup easier at the conclusion of a session. Many child therapists find a cork bulletin board useful for hanging the paintings that children produce, for "posting" the scores of games played, and even for hanging pictures appropriate for the season of the year. A wall mounted chalkboard is also used for chalk art productions and scorekeeping.

FAMILY AND GROUP THERAPY ROOM

If your practice will include family and/or group therapy in addition to individual therapy, you may choose to use your own office as the site of these sessions. This may not, though, be the best idea. Because of the physical requirements necessitated by the larger groups, the desired intimacy of the individual therapeutic approach may be lost. Hence, you should give serious thought to a separate room to be used exclusively for groups and families.

This room should be comfortable and appropriately furnished. Ordinarily, couches should not be used if you are seeing adults only for the same reason described in the section on waiting room furniture. However, this may be an individual matter for the professional in terms of theoretical orientation. The main factors to consider are comfort and equal visibility. Do not position seats so that a table lamp will obscure one group member from another. If you permit smoking, ashtrays will be needed. If you serve refreshments, coffee/cocktail tables with mar-proof surfaces can be enormously helpful. A box of tissues can be a considerate touch by the therapist.

If your practice is exclusively family and/or group therapy, you may feel that you don't want or need an office plus a therapy room. In that case, all of the above applies, but you will also have to provide your own personal non-patient-contact working space within the room design. This can be done in a variety of ways, including installing a modular unit with a fold-down desk or simply placing your working desk in an unobtrusive corner of the room. Since you will be seeing numbers of people at the same time, special care should be taken for the preservation of confidential materials.

SECRETARIAL SPACE

Secretarial space requires all of the usual equipment used

by a secretary/typist/receptionist. It should be comfortable, utilitarian, and visible. Office personnel ordinarily require a special desk with typewriter compartment, typist's chair, and ready access to current files and all the forms that might possibly be needed in a day's work. Using a secretary/receptionist will allow you the luxury of a buzz on the phone to tell you of the arrival of your next appointment, rather than running out into the waiting room to see if they've arrived yet. The telephone company will be glad to consult with you and advise as to the best kind of service for your needs.

5

Running the Office:
Nuts and Bolts

You have made the decision to go into private practice and selected the office and furnishings—now all you have to do is sit near the phone and wait for the flood of referrals. Right? Wrong!

Now we must look into all the important details, the nuts and bolts of running the office in the most efficient way so that you can conduct the professional part of your practice with minimal intrusion from the operational necessities.

ANSWERING THE TELEPHONE

The telephone will prove to be an important adjunct to the practice and is more fully discussed in Chapter 6. However, an important part of telephone service involves who answers the telephone and how it is answered when no one is in the office.

If you have either full- or part-time office help, they, of course, will do the answering, but you must determine just how much responsibility you want to devolve upon them. Some practitioners permit their secretaries full latitude in making the initial telephone contact and allow them to make the first appointment for patients. Others feel that the psycho-chologist should handle that aspect of patient relationships and will take all such calls and make all initial appointments. This must be determined by your own philosophy and your own needs.

But how will your phone be answered when no one is there? There are two general options: the live telephone answering service, or the electronic answering machine. Since there are positive and negative features to both answering methods, the final choice is an individual matter.

Answering Service

The live telephone answering service will have an extension line connected from your office to theirs. When the phone in your office rings, so will theirs. The fee for the telephone line will be added to your monthly telephone bill, as will the initial installation charge. In addition, you will pay the answering service a monthly fee in return for which your phone will be answered for you while the office is vacant and, if you choose, while you are with patients. The answering service may arrange with you to answer on the first ring or wait, for example, until it has rung four times (to make certain they should answer) before coming in on your line. They will answer the phone in any way you choose, e.g., "Dr. Jones' office," or just by giving your telephone number.

The advantage to this method is that a live human being answers the phone and can often be helpful in answering questions, sometimes helpful in assuaging patients' anxiety, and can also reach you quickly in an emergency (providing you have told them where to reach you and that you want to be reached). Most people prefer to have a real, live human being to relate to, even if it is just someone from the answering service. If you choose to utilize the answering service, it is wise to visit them and discuss with them the needs of your practice. They should be told, for example, just how you want the phone answered and also that there may be times when a sympathetic ear will be required on their part. Also, you may, from time to time, want to give them the name of a particular patient about whom you are concerned and tell them to reach you immediately if that patient calls.

If you prefer not to answer the phone while with patients and don't want to be annoyed by the ringing, the telephone company can adjust your set so that you can turn off the bell and it will ring only at the office of your answering service.

What are the disadvantages to an answering service? Many answering services, during busy times of the day, just can't answer as quickly as they should. It is not unusual to have patients complain that the phone rang 20 times without being answered, and that they finally hung up in disgust. Also, the person answering the phone may have had a bad day and just may not be able to respond with the appropriate kind of warmth and understanding needed for a person in crisis. And, of course, there are mistakes—the answering service has been known to write down the incorrect number or put your messages in the wrong pigeonhole so that the plumber down the street gets your calls.

Electronic Answering Machines

This kind of device provides instant, totally reliable answering of your phone. It will answer it after the first ring, and it never has a bad day, never gets depressed, and never gets annoyed with callers. Many of the current models are equipped so that you can call the machine from your home phone, other place of work or, for that matter, from any place in the world, and get your messages relayed to you over the wires. They can be adjusted so that, when you use this remote system to get calls, your machine will automatically erase all the previous messages and start anew, or they can be set to accumulate and replay everything on the tape each time you call in. You can then erase all the material when you return to the office. Some of the machines can even be signaled to replay the tape should you be unsure about one or another of the messages you have just taken.

With these machines, the message you leave for callers is very important. Ordinarily, you should introduce yourself, apologize for the use of a machine, and then give instructions for leaving a message. A sample message for such a machine is as follows: "This is Dr. Jones. I'm sorry that this is a recorded message, but I'm unable to answer the phone at the moment. When you hear the tone, please leave your name, number, and any message you wish to, and I will call you back shortly. Thank you for calling." At the conclusion of the message, the caller will hear an electronic "beep" and can then leave a message of any length desired.

Additionally, some of these machines have a device where, through the use of the remote control feature, you can change the message from another phone. Thus, if you want patients to call you at another number, you can call your machine and prepare such a message. One final advantage of these devices is that you don't have to answer the phone when you are otherwise occupied, if you choose not to. If you are alone but don't wish to answer the phone, you can turn up the volume control, allow the machine to answer, monitor the call, and then decide if you want to talk to the insurance salesman—or the patient in distress.

There are only two disadvantages to using the electronic answering machine. Many people either don't like to talk to a machine or else are made anxious by the necessity of doing so. Additionally, many professionals don't like having their patients talk to a machine.

There are also two possible problems with the electronic answering device. The first is the "crank call." Children, for example, sometimes discover that you have that wonderful machine and, on rainy weekends, may spend a diverting few minutes calling you. Most of the time they will stop after discovering that there is really minimal gratification to be derived from talking to a machine that doesn't answer. However, if the calls persist or fall into the category of "obscene calls," the telephone company can quickly determine their source and take appropriate action.

The other possible problem is that of coverage while you are away from the area. If you use the answering service you can make arrangements with a colleague to "cover" emergencies for you while you are gone, and patients can be referred to him. With the answering machine this is, of course, not possible. The practitioner, by and large, knows his caseload, and any patients who may encounter difficulty can be given the name and number of an available colleague before the psychologist goes away. The colleague, in turn, should, of course, be alerted to the possibility of such a call.

Call Forwarding

This is a relatively new service that the telephone companies have instituted in some areas of the country. It can be used by itself or as an adjunct to either of the two answering methods already described. This service permits you to program your office telephone, when you are away, so that all calls will automatically ring at a different, preselected number. Thus, you can receive office calls at home, at a gathering in a friend's home (they'll *love* that), or at your weekend vacation retreat (*you'll* love that). However, it can help, and does work.

There can also be a bonus to the call forwarding system.

You can set your home phone to ring at the office and then your answering service or answering machine can take your personal calls when you are away.

The drawback to this system, of course, is that you cannot possibly be close to a telephone 24 hours a day and, in private practice, the phone must be available on a 24-hour-a-day basis. So it would seem that you must realistically make the choice between the human answering service with its drawbacks or the electronic answering device with its drawbacks.

Another new service of the telephone company allows you the benefits of two telephone lines while only having one. That is, if someone else dials your number while you are already on the phone, you will receive an electronic signal and can then put the first party on "hold" while answering the new caller.

Classified Listings—Where

Part of your telephone service is the Yellow Page listing which is discussed in Chapter 6. But where do you put your listing? That is, should you only list in the directory covering the geographic area where your office is located or should you list in other directories in your area as well? In a metropolitan area with one directory, it is ordinarily sufficient to have the one listing, especially if your office is located in the downtown area. However, in a metropolitan area like New York City, for example, which has a number of directories, it might be advisable to list in each of them. Certainly, if you practice in a suburban or rural area it is a good idea to take a Yellow Page listing in the areas contiguous with the one in which you maintain your office.

Classified Listings—How

In addition to the "Psychologists" listings, you may also choose to list yourself under other headings *if you qualify*. In other words, if you are also a certified marriage and family counselor, for example, you could use this category of listings as well.

Whatever headings you use for listings it is ordinarily appropriate to use name, highest appropriate degree, the designation "ABPP" (if appropriate), as well as the limitations of your practice, if any.

ANSWERING THE MAIL

In most practices there is an ongoing need for some kind of secretarial/typing services. The largely psychodiagnostic/ consulting practice needs more, of course, than does the practice which is primarily psychotherapeutic in nature. But the need is there, too, in terms of correspondence and, possibly, typing of therapy notes. Certainly, when the practice deals with children, there are all of the usual written communications necessary with schools, pediatricians, etc. And there are always the teachers, guidance counselors, and others involved with the child who want to hear from you and receive written reports. Preparation of these written materials can be time-consuming, but they are necessary for the proper, ethical conduct of a practice—and they also make for good relationships with others in the overall professional community.

Employees

What varieties of services are available to you? In general, there are four different options available. You can hire a full-time secretary/receptionist. You can find a part-time person to do this work for you. You may decide to utilize the services of a do-it-at-home typist. Or, finally, you may opt to do your own typing or have your spouse do it for you. Each of these options has both advantages and disadvantages, and we'll try to explore them all.

Full-Time Employee. Ideally, one might want a full-time secretary/receptionist. This would be someone who would be in the office all through the working day, whether or not you are there. This employee would answer the phone, make appointments, greet arriving patients, keep the books, do the billing, type the correspondence, fill out the insurance forms, make the morning coffee, and even provide animated conversation when a patient has canceled or there is a blank spot in the schedule. This is the ideal, and if you go this route your life will be a lot easier. Also, if you go this route, you will, of course, have to make physical provision in your office for such an employee (see Chapter 4).

The professional psychologist must be especially careful in the selection of office personnel because of the confidential and often sensitive nature of the materials that the secretary will be typing. Therefore, a mature, perceptive individual must be found, and the practitioner should feel free to interview in order to probe for that maturity. The need for absolute confidentiality must be stressed, and the new employee should also be evaluated for typing/filing skills by using some of the clerical tests available through the various firms publishing testing materials.

In hiring a full-time employee one must be prepared for the various legal and moral responsibilities to paid personnel. There will be income tax to be withheld, along with unemployment insurance, social security, and workmen's compensation payments. These will, of course, entail both careful record keeping and governmental forms to be completed at regular intervals. If you are incorporated, you will also have to make provisions for participation in whatever retirement plans you may have as part of your corporation. Finally, provision will have to be made for paid sick leave, vacation time and, perhaps, temporary personnel while your secretary is away. (Many practitioners solve this latter problem by arranging to close the office for vacation so that all are away at the same time.)

The full-time employee is, indeed, the ideal arrangement— if you need one. A competent secretary can remove most of the burden of running the office, and permits one to really devote full-time attention to the professional aspects of the practice. The drawbacks are the costs involved, the need for additional space, and, finally, the discomfort that some patients might feel (especially in small communities) about being "seen" by a non-professional person in your office.

Part-Time Employee. Hiring a part-time secretary/receptionist provides about the same benefits as does hiring a full-time employee and presents about the same problems. The major difference, of course, is the diminished expense of salary, which is equaled by the diminished availability and familiarity with your office routines and procedures. It is sometimes easier to find a mature part-time employee, though, because there are many competent women whose families are raised and who now want part-time work.

The Do-It-At-Home-Typist. Many practitioners feel that they have no real need for an employee in the office and find that they can function best when they are truly alone there. Their needs for typing may be such that they can utilize the services of one of the many highly capable people who contract to do typing in their own homes, using their own equipment. In such an instance the psychologist will ordinarily utilize a dictating machine and separate transcribing unit. Material is dictated and collected, usually on a weekly basis, by the typist, who then transcribes it and returns the typed material in a few days. Fees charged for this type of service are ordinarily on an hourly or per-page basis.

Such services are usually available in even the smallest of communities, and ads offering them are usually found in the classified columns of local newspapers. If none such appear, placing your own classified ad will ordinarily produce a flood of calls. It is, of course, important to interview any person who will be handling your typing to be sure that he or she is mature, discrete and reliable. A final advantage to utilizing the services of such an independent contractor is that there are no involvements with income tax, social security, etc.

Secretary Sharing. If you are in a space sharing arrangement with a colleague, you may also be able to share a secretary in terms of time and expenses. In this case it is important to make certain that you both can agree on what kind of person you want to hire, what his/her responsibilities will be to each of you, to whom he/she is responsible in the administrative sense, and how you will share the expenses. Again, as in other, similar issues, all this should be adequately clarified *before* someone is hired and, if possible, be in writing.

On the other hand, if you are renting space from an established professional, you may be able to utilize the services of the secretarial personnel already on the scene as part of your overall rental arrangement. Unless the lessor is also a mental health professional, you may have to take special pains to instruct the secretary in your confidentiality requirements as well as in your professional vocabulary. This arrangement should be clear before your final rental arrangements are made and, of course, in writing as part of the lease arrangement.

Temporary Personnel. Still another solution to the need for typing services is the use of temporary personnel from agencies like "Kelly Girls," or "Manpower, Inc." These agencies can usually provide highly skilled typists who can, according to your needs, copy your handwritten or typed material, take dictation, or use your transcribing machine. You will have to provide all the equipment and a place to work, since they come to your office. These personnel can be called upon on an "as needed" basis, limiting your expenses. There are two disadvantages to the use of these agencies. First, they are ordinarily quite expensive, as compared with the other services described. Second, using them ordinarily means close supervision of the typist each time in terms of technical usage and your own unique system of reports and correspondence. Rarely will the same typist be sent to your office each time you call the agency. However, these agencies can be extremely helpful at times when your regular employee is ill or on vacation. They can also be used if you encounter a sudden flood of referrals temporarily requiring clerical work beyond the capacity of your regular employee.

Do-It-Yourself. Finally, many beginning practitioners decide to either do their own typing or else enlist the aid of their spouse. While it may appear that this saves money, it really may become quite expensive in the long run. Your time, after all, is the real commodity that you are "selling," and the time it takes to do your own typing should be put to better use. It may well be that your spouse's time is also valuable and should be utilized for other things. Further, unless you or your spouse is an expert, professional typist, you should consider carefully before attempting to do your own typing. The materials that leave your office over your signature should have a finished, professional look to them. A well typed letter or report adds to the professional aura of the material you are sending. And, conversely, poorly typed materials may lead the recipient to wonder at your professionalism and at your real commitment to private practice. This, whether we like it or not, is the reality. People, even other professionals, look at "the package."

FORMS AND SUPPLIES

The letterhead you write on should be neat, attractive, appropriate, and ethical. Letterhead stationery should ordi-

FIGURE 1

CLINICAL PSYCHOLOGY   BY APPOINTMENT

ALVIN MYLES JONES, Ph.D.
965 WALT WHITMAN ROAD
MELVILLE, N. Y. 11746
TELEPHONE 421-1200

narily carry your name, highest relevant degree, diplomate status (if appropriate), address, and telephone. It may also carry a description of your specific professional activity, e.g. "Clinical Psychology," "Consulting Psychologist," etc.

The illustration in Figure 1 is that of a standard, traditional letterhead. Many practitioners have letterhead especially designed, using colored paper and colored ink. This, again, is an individual matter. Although the individually designed letterhead is ordinarily more expensive than the traditional, it can be extremely attractive and gratifying to the ego; it is also "noticed" by the people receiving it.

The usual size is 8½ by 11 inches for the paper, with a corresponding No. 10 envelope. Some practitioners also have a smaller size letterhead which they use for brief notes. The amount you order will, of course, be determined by the volume of correspondence leaving your office. Most stationers print in multiples of 500 sheets and envelopes and, while this should be more than enough to get you started, you can save some future dollars by ordering more.

Billheads are also standard items (see Figure 2). Here, again, you may choose to use a unique design. Billheads may be utilized in a number of ways. Some, like the one illustrated, are folded and inserted into a window envelope of appropriate size. Others are totally self contained. That is, the bill is part of the envelope which, in turn, becomes the envelope in which the patient places the check to return to you. Still another method of billing involves the use of a special record keeping card which is then photocopied and placed in a window envelope. And there are other billing systems, as well. The key is to find one with which you are comfortable and which meets the needs of your practice.

One final word about letterhead and billhead. The greatest tongue/saliva saver in the world is the self-sealing envelope.

If you plan on a practice in which you will be doing

FIGURE 2

STATEMENT

Telephone 421-1200

ALVIN MYLES JONES, Ph.D.
965 WALT WHITMAN ROAD
MELVILLE, N. Y. 11746

_____19___

_____

_____

_____

FOR PROFESSIONAL SERVICES:

psychodiagnostic evaluations, it is a good idea to use a special form for that purpose. A discussion and example of such a form appear in Chapter 7.

You will need appointment cards for your patients as well as professional cards. The appointment card is discussed in Chapter 8, but one preliminary point should be made here. It is usually a good idea to send an appointment card to a patient who has called for a first visit. It helps confirm the date and time and, if you use the kind of card that indicates a fee charged for broken appointments, will either assist the patient's motivation or will produce a phone call, in advance, advising of the cancellation. Professional cards, similar to the one illustrated in Figure 3, can be carried in the wallet, left

FIGURE 3

ALVIN MYLES JONES, Ph.D.
CLINICAL PSYCHOLOGY

TELEPHONE   965 WALT WHITMAN ROAD
421-1200   MELVILLE, N. Y. 11746

in a holder in the waiting room, and kept in a desk drawer. Many times you will encounter someone who will want your card for later contact, or a colleague (read that to mean "potential source of referral") will ask for a card. People in the waiting room often like to take a card with them—they then have your number readily available; perhaps it also means that they are taking a symbolic representation of you along with them. Unfortunately, if you see many children in your practice, you will find that kids see these cards as great playthings.

You will, of course, need a folder for each patient you see. The ordinary, "third cut" manila folder is adequate. This is a manila folder with the top tab placed in three different positions in each box of one hundred. Thus, when put in a file drawer, all the names will not be one behind the other and will be easier to locate. Of course, you will need at least one or two file cabinets at the beginning. It is best to buy good ones with the drawers on rollers. Once they begin to fill up—and they will—it is easier to pull out this kind of drawer for easy access. Also, the file cabinets should have locks for purposes of safety and confidentiality. If your new office has a separate area for storage, this would be a good place for the file cabinets.

Beginning with the first patient you see in the office, you will need a quick and readily accessible source of name, address, and telephone number. You will also need a record of fees paid, owed, and visits made. The best single way to accomplish this is to keep a separate account card, which contains all that data, for each patient. Such a card, like the one shown in Figure 4, is a ready reference which also simplifies monthly billing. As you will note, it contains most of the very basic "face sheet" information, along with a running record of the financial status of each individual case. These cards should be kept in a small file box in a desk drawer. It's a good idea to discipline yourself, very early, to make the appropriate entry either just before or just after each visit. As a double check on yourself, it is also helpful to make a check mark, in your appointment book, after the patient's name, following each visit. In fact, the simpler and easier the system, the simpler and easier the nuts and bolts of the practice will be.

FIGURE 4

(———————————————)   ——————————————————
PATIENT'S NAME AND CASE NO.   CHARGE TO

ADDRESS_____TEL. NO._____REFERRED BY_____

INSURANCE _____

DATE	DESCRIPTION	CHARGE	PAID	BALANCE	DATE	DESCRIPTION	CHARGE	PAID	BALANCE

You will also need a ledger in which to enter your receipts. This can be a simple, small book called "Single Entry Ledger" which can be found at all stationers. It will contain a record of all of your cash receipts (checks are also considered cash). Most practitioners find that a monthly record, kept on a daily basis, will suffice. In this way you will have an accurate, easy to read record of the exact amount of money you have received at any point of the week, month, or year. It will also make it a lot easier for your accountant when he audits your books and prepares a statement on the actual state of your practice. An accurate record of your cash flow will, when compared with your expenditures, tell him, and you, precisely how you are doing and help in the projection of your estimated income taxes.

The appointment book is sometimes referred to as the practitioner's bible. This is the book that tells you whom you have seen, whom you are about to see, and whom you may see next week or next month. It will tell you where you have to go and where you have been. It can be used as a record for cash disbursements that you may otherwise forget. Many appointment books have a place in the back of the book that can be used for listing the names and telephone numbers of all of your current case load—which you may need in case an emergency keeps you unexpectedly away from the office and you have to contact patients in a hurry.

One of the best kinds of appointment books for all of these purposes is about eight by ten inches (closed), shows appointments at 15-minute intervals through the evening hours, and, when open, permits you to see an entire week's schedule at once. Even though you may schedule your appointments at essentially the same times, the 15-minute breakdown gives you additional flexibility. It is especially useful for those practitioners who schedule appointments for 40 or 45 minutes, with little or no break between visits.

There are also smaller size appointment books available that will fit easily into a coat pocket or purse. The only real disadvantages to these books are the size, which limits the amount of writing one can put on the lines provided, and the fact that they are usually divided into hourly or half hourly, rather than quarterly, subdivisions.

You will also need two kinds of authorization or permission forms, which, when signed by a patient or parent, will either permit you to release information about a case or permit some other professional, agency, or school to release information to you. The form can be a simple statement on a piece of paper which states either, *"I authorize.............................to release information concerning (my) (my child.........................) case to Dr. A. M. Jones,"* or *"I authorize Dr. A. M. Jones to release information concerning (my) (my child....................) case to ...."* Each form should provide specific space for signature and address, along with the date signed. These forms can be duplicated, at very nominal cost, at almost any of the "instant printing" shops that abound.

Another form that is needed, but usually not as often as others, is a receipt blank for those patients who pay their bill in cash or for those who would like a receipt in addition to their canceled check. Most practitioners find that there are relatively few cash transactions, but a receipt form is a good, businesslike way of handling these. It should be a standard form, imprinted with your name and address. Here, again, there are a choice of varieties. Some of the forms are merely single, original copies, while others come with a second sheet of NCR paper or carbon paper, so that you have a record of receipts written.

Mention of cash receipts brings up the question of what to do with such monies. The usual inclination of most of us is to record the receipt in the ledger and then place the cash in the pocket. This is a poor practice and may create potential problems with the Internal Revenue Service. It is also a good way to give your accountant gray hair and ulcers.

All receipts, check or cash, should be placed in the office checking account. All monies taken from the practice, for whatever purpose, should be written as checks. Then, your receipts and disbursements will balance exactly, and IRS can raise no questions about unaccounted for monies. It's a bit more trouble, but worth the effort in the long run.

The office checking account, incidentally, should be just that. Many practitioners use one account for both personal and office expenses, and that system can work. However, the most efficient way to handle your office banking business is via a separate account used only for office receipts and disbursements. The monies you take from the practice for your personal expenses will then fall under the category of "disbursement," and can be so accounted for in later auditing by your accountant. In this way there is no blurring of expendi-

FIGURE 5

ALVIN MYLES JONES, Ph.D.
965 Walt Whitman Road
Melville, N. Y. 11746

School Report Form

Will you please provide us with the information requested on this form plus any additional data and/or information you might feel would help in our further understanding of this child. A release of information form, signed by the parent or legal guardian, is enclosed. It would be most helpful if this form could be filled out by both teacher and principal, cooperatively.

Date............................

Name of Child.......................................B.D...............C.A............

Address ....

School ....Grade................

Name of Teacher ....

Name of Principal ....

Has this child been retained in any grades? If yes, please give grades and details.

Is this child working up to grade level? Above? Below? Please detail.

Does he (she) have many friends in class? Is he (she) accepted by the other children? Please detail.

What has been your impression of the parents in relation to the school? Have they, for example, been cooperative or non-cooperative, interested or disinterested, etc.

Please use the space below to give the results of psychometric and/or educational tests that have been administered, with dates.

Please use the space below for a summary of any psychological reports or, more preferably, attach a copy of the full psychological report to this form.

Please use the space below for any additional comments, information, or professional opinions you may have that would be of help in our work with this youngster.

tures, there is a clear-cut record of receipts, and income versus expenditures will clearly balance for your accountant and for the IRS man who may audit your books. Additionally, it is a good idea to keep, in chronological order, all paid bills and receipts for any office expense. If they have been paid via check, it is also a good idea to write on the face of the bill the check number with which it was paid and the date paid.

If your practice will include children you may well want information from schools concerning youngsters whom you are seeing, especially at the very beginning of the relationship when you need information about overall school adjustment. Schools, unhappily, do not always respond in the way that we would wish them to when they receive a request for information. They will very often send a photocopy of the last report card, along with the Iowa scores—and that's all. This may occur even when you ask for anecdotal material. Thus, a "School Report Form" can be very helpful. Such a form should be structured to provide answers to the kinds of questions you would like answered, along with space for the teacher or principal to offer any more information that they may think relevant. The sample form shown in Figure 5 is a guide to the way such a form can be developed. When writing to a school for information, a covering letter, a school report form, and a signed authorization form make a neat, ethical "package" that will usually produce the results you want in terms of additional information about a child.

Mention was made earlier of dictating machines. They can be extremely useful whether or not you have a full- or part-time employee. They permit you to "talk your thoughts" directly when doing clinical notes, and they allow you the luxury of preparing written material without first laboriously writing by hand or typing "hunt and peck" fashion. Most manufacturers produce both the dictating machine itself, which you use, and the transcriber, which your typist uses.

Most machines use one kind or another of tape cassettes. There are, though, two basic kinds of machines. One is the standard, desk top office model which is designed to stay on your desk and which is not really portable. The transcribing unit accompanying it is usually also a desk size model. These machines are usually quite versatile in terms of having replay devices, tapes for indicating where and what you have dictated, etc. The other general type of dictating machine is the portable variety. Portable dictating units are usually small enough to put in an attaché case or even your pocket. The accompanying transcriber is also smaller than the usual desk model. These machines, while versatile, do not have the wide range of features found in the desk models. However, their greatest merit lies in their portability. With the smaller machine it is easier to bring work home, dictate, and either bring the tape cassette back to the office or give it to the typist who works at home.

None of these machines is really inexpensive (although the portable units cost less, generally, than do the others), but a dictating/transcribing unit can be a sound investment that can free you for the professional aspects of your practice. Since there are many such machines on the market, it is best to invite salesmen to call on you so that you can determine which one best meets your needs.

KEEPING THE PLACE CLEAN

Keeping the office clean is still another of the nuts and bolts kinds of things that can make life just a bit easier for the practitioner if properly handled. The impulse, when first beginning a practice, is to try to do as much as you can yourself, in order to cut down on expenses. But, as with so many other facets of practice, it may well be a case of being penny wise and pound foolish. The actual mechanics of cleaning the office, washing the toilet bowl, and polishing the desk are all dirty work. It's not much fun, and it takes time. This is time that you should be using for other purposes and, if you consider the fees you charge, cleaning the office is a very expensive way of utilizing that time.

There are businesses that specialize in office cleaning, and they will come into your office, with their own equipment, at prearranged times when you are not there. They can go through your office like a pack of elves, leaving no dirt in their wake, and you will have a clean, well kept place in which to work. Their fees, of course, vary from locale to locale, but a few calls will yield the information you need. How often you will need them will depend on the amount of traffic through your office. Most practitioners find that once every week or two is sufficient for a good general cleaning. Then, all you will have to do is empty ashtrays and wastepaper baskets before you leave at night—that, and a quick spray with an aerosol room freshener, and you are all set for the next morning's operations.

SPENDING MONEY

It seems reasonable, at this point, to insert a thought or two about money. Not the money you will make, but the money this and other chapters have suggested you must spend in order to go into private practice.

Most small businesses that don't make it fail because they are undercapitalized. In a genuine sense, a private practice is a small business. You have property, either rented or owned. You have equipment—furnishings and test materials. And you have "wares"—yourself. But there is no need to enter practice in a state of undercapitalization. If you don't have sufficient savings to open your office on your own, don't be afraid to seek out your local banking institution. As with mortgage money, most banks are delighted to lend you the money you will need for the "nut" required to go into practice. Ordinarily they have had this experience with other beginning professionals and they will be glad to both advise you and lend you the money you need. They will also arrange a repayment schedule that is realistic for your particular circumstances. Finally, the interest you will pay on such a loan is fully deductible from your income taxes as a legitimate business expense. So, don't be put off by the dollar signs dancing before your eyes; the money is there and will be available to you.

INSURANCE

Finally, a brief note about insurance. While insurance and insurance men will be discussed in Chapter 9, one or two things should be mentioned here as part of running the office.

Make certain that you have everything insured—furnishings, books, equipment, pictures on the wall . . . everything. And make certain that your coverage is for theft and fire. It is not unusual for offices to be burglarized any more than it is unusual for fires to occur. You need the protection and it is usually relatively inexpensive.

Insuring everything also means insuring *yourself*. Don't neglect to take out professional liability insurance (usually called malpractice insurance). We live in a society that is increasingly litigation minded, and the saddest words in the language may well be those of the practicing professional who said, "It couldn't happen to me."

6

Getting Started: Referral Sources

Although we may assume that you are not going into practice "cold" and that you already have a patient or two (or more), it is still vital that you develop a broad base of possible referral sources that will "feed" your growing practice. This chapter will give you some ideas about how to become known and how to develop these referral sources. Without them, you have no practice! Because we are ethical practitioners who do not, as yet, advertise, we depend upon others for our patients.

Become known in your own profession. Your colleagues should know you and be aware that you are in practice or, at least, are planning to enter practice very soon. Join all of the local professional societies and become active. Volunteer for committees and be prepared to take on some of the lower level jobs at first. You will become known as a worker, you will become known as a professional who is involved in the profession, and, most important of all, you will become *known*. Additionally, you will be making a contribution to your profession. This work will probably not produce a flood of referrals, but when referral sources are needed, your colleagues will remember you. Also, when prospective patients inquire about you (and many do), you will not just be an unknown name or a listing in a directory.

Send out announcements that meet the ethical requirements of the American Psychological Association. They may list your name, highest appropriate degree, office address and telephone numbers, and office hours or, if you prefer, the statement "by appointment only." You may also briefly indicate the kind of service you are prepared to offer, e.g., "psychodiagnosis and psychotherapy," or "behavior therapy," etc. (see Figure 6). The American Psychological Association now also permits the inclusion of a statement regarding your fee structure, if you wish.

The announcement should be sent to all appropriate professionals, agencies, and schools. Physicians, attorneys, dentists, and clergymen are all potential sources of referral. Local mental health associations, university psychology clinics and counseling services, and college departments of psychology should also be on the mailing list. All local agencies, includ-

FIGURE 6

ALVIN MYLES JONES, PH.D.

ANNOUNCES THE OPENING OF HIS OFFICE FOR
THE PRACTICE OF CLINICAL PSYCHOLOGY

AT

965 WALT WHITMAN ROAD
MELVILLE, N. Y. 11746

OFFICE HOURS
BY APPOINTMENT

TELEPHONE
421-1200

ing mental health clinics, cerebral palsy clinics, mental retardation facilities, family counseling services, etc., should be advised of your entry into practice.

It may be possible in the area in which you are about to practice to also place an announcement in the local newspaper. This, ordinarily, is a matter of local custom. In other words, if other professionals do it, you may, as well. If they don't, you should not either. The same information should be included as in the mailed announcement. If you do place an announcement in a newspaper, it should be for the customary length of time in your locale.

When you open your office and obtain telephone service it will ordinarily be "business service" which will entitle you to a Yellow Page listing. This, according to ethical standards, may be your name and highest relevant degree. You may list a specialty only if, indeed, you are limiting your practice to the areas you list. The description "children, adolescents, and adults" is *not* a practice-limiting statement and is considered unethical. Try, if possible, to arrange for telephone service before the closing date for listings in the Yellow Pages. Most practitioners do, indeed, get "Yellow Page referrals" throughout the year. While it is an unwise way for the prospective patient to seek out the services of a professional, it does happen—and you might as well be available to take advantage of it. Besides, potential patients may have heard of you but have no idea where you practice or how to reach you, so that the listing is simply convenient for prospective patients.

After sending out your announcements, contact the local mental health association and other community direct service agencies to find out if they have referral lists. Many do and will be glad to have a new resource to whom they can send referrals. These agencies ordinarily give the caller a list of three names of qualified professionals, from which the prospective patient can select one.

City, county, and state agencies very often are in need of qualified professionals to provide diagnostic and, sometimes, therapeutic service. The State office which administers Supplemental Social Income (Social Security), for example, frequently requires psychological evaluations as part of the decision-making process in a given case. State rehabilitation commissions need these same services, as do the state agencies responsible for various kinds of children's services and local welfare boards. A letter to the director of these agencies will usually produce an application form which will result in your being named to a panel of qualified psychologists to whom cases are referred.

One of the best, fastest, and easiest ways to become known in your community is to be available for speaking engagements. List yourself with the speakers bureau of your professional society and with the mental health association. All through the year (except the summer months), there are organizations that need a "program." For better or for worse, we live in an age where the mental health professional is in great demand for these programs. You will find yourself talking to such diverse groups as PTA's, single parents groups, and your local service clubs (Kiwanis, Rotary, etc.).

It is ordinarily a good idea to find out from the program chairman, when you are contacted about the engagement, just what they would like you to talk about. Doing this will ordinarily elicit a subject that is close to the hearts of the group while, at the same time, it demonstrates to them that you care enough to understand their interests. Besides, it also makes one feel a little less like a "program," and more like a speaker whom they really want to hear!

Always go to such engagements well prepared. A recent survey of an ongoing lecture series featuring a different speaker each month for five months revealed that the single factor producing the most negative comments about speakers was that some did not come prepared. The comments conveyed the feeling that even though these speakers obviously knew their subject, the audience felt denigrated because the professional didn't think enough of the occasion to prepare for it ahead of time.

Not only should one go to a speaking engagement prepared, but one should also prepare the group for the speaker. One way is to send the program chairman a curriculum vitae in advance with a note explaining your awareness that they might wish the information for their pre-program publicity. Providing such information also helps in how you are introduced on the night of the talk. You don't really want the introduction to go, "Uh, this is Dr., uh, Jones. I think she's a psychologist, or a psychiatrist, or something like that."

Finally, going prepared to a speaking engagement and sending a curriculum vitae in advance is an ethical way of obtaining public awareness of your existence and the kinds of things you do. Speaking engagements often produce referrals —sometimes a year after the night you spoke.

Ultimately, of course, your referral sources will include former patients. They will tell others about the positive experiences they have had with you and will be delighted to refer people to you. Many practitioners discover, after some years of practice, that their most productive sources of referrals are former patients.

It should be evident, by now, that developing sources of referral is a matter that must be carefully planned and executed. When this is done, the referrals will surely follow. There is rarely a flood of patients at the beginning of any practice; it is the rare professional who finds the appointment book completely filled in the first months after opening the office. But a careful, reasonable approach to the development of sources of referral will work, and the practice will work, and so, ultimately will you work—and work hard.

7

The Care and Feeding
of Referral Sources

We have already discussed the various ways of developing sources of referral. Maintaining good relations with referral sources is, in fact, an ongoing need which will continue throughout the life of your practice. Sources of referral are rarely permanent, no matter how good the relationship between you and the professionals who send you cases. The only reason cases should be sent to you is because the referral source is convinced that you can do the best job for that patient. If you don't do the job well, your sources will hear about it and turn elsewhere. This is true for all of the practicing professions and is one of the facts of professional life. So, it is in your best interest to provide adequate nurturing for those who think enough of you to send cases. In other words, it is your responsibility to yourself, in terms of the growth and development of your practice, to be able to demonstrate to your sources of referral that they have made the correct decision in referring cases to you.

Two basic legs upon which the maintenance of referrals stands are *relationship* and *communication*. Any time a case has been referred to you it is a good idea to contact the source of referral with the information that the case has, indeed, been seen. This should be done quite soon after the initial contact and can be either a telephone call or a brief note. Even the busiest professional appreciates a call, and all are glad to know that the patient has followed through. The first call or letter can simply indicate that the patient has been seen for initial visit and what your immediate plans may be; it should, of course, include some expression of thanks for the referral. Figure 7 is a typical initial communication with a referral source.

Once some disposition has been made of the case, there should be another contact with the referral source. This should be a letter in greater detail than the initial communication. If it is to be, for example, a treatment case, you should advise the referral source of your impressions of the patient, your plans for therapy, and, perhaps, about how long you think you may be seeing the patient. If you choose to call first, you should still follow up with this detailed letter. Then the referring professional can file your letter with other data about the patient. Additionally, this detailed letter also reinforces awareness of *you* and your efficiency in handling his referrals.

If the case is a consultation, then, of course, a highly detailed written report is indicated. It is of critical importance, in the development of a successful practice, to send out your consultation reports at the earliest possible time. There have been many very competent practitioners who have lost referral sources just because they have been too casual about prompt transmission of consultation data. You have, after all, been consulted because the referring professional has questions about the patient which you are expected to answer. Promptness of response is not only courteous, but it may well be essential in the overall management of the case by the referring source.

CLINICAL PSYCHOLOGY   BY APPOINTMENT

ALVIN MYLES JONES, Ph.D.
865 WALT WHITMAN ROAD
MELVILLE, N. Y. 11746

TELEPHONE 421-1200

8 September 1978

Joseph P. Braun, M.D.
30 Garden State Drive
Somewhere, New Jersey   RF: KIDD, James D.
                                       B.D. 6/12/68

Dear Dr. Braun:

I have had a preliminary meeting with Mr. & Mrs. Kidd,
parents of James, who you were kind enough to refer because of his ongoing behavioral difficulties.

In my meeting with the parents there was sufficient evid-
ence, from the history that I took, that James, indeed,
may be experiencing serious emotional difficulties. As a
result, I plan on seeing him for a series of psychological
examinations. I shall also contact the school so they can
provide me with detailed information about his school performance and behavior.

If, at the conclusion of these studies, I feel that James
is in need of psychotherapy I shall suggest to the parents
that I see him on a regular basis.

I will schedule an interpretive conference with Mr. and
Mrs. Kidd when the studies are completed and I have heard
from the school. Following that meeting I will send you
a summary of my findings and recommendations. Thank you
for your confidence in referring this most interesting
child.

Sincerely yours,

Alvin Myles Jones, Ph.D.

AMJ:pbs

The consultation report may be on your regular letterhead
or you may choose to design a "Report of Psychological Examination" form of your own. The sample form in Figure 8 is
one that has been used for some years. The use of such a form
makes it clear that this is a consultation report. The basic
identifying data are clearly visible. A colored paper of heavy

FIGURE 8

ALVIN MYLES JONES, Ph.D.
965 WALT WHITMAN ROAD
MELVILLE, N. Y. 11746
—
TELEPHONE: 421-1200

REPORT OF PSYCHOLOGICAL EXAMINATION

NAME: DATE(S) SEEN:

BIRTH DATE: AGE: REFERRED BY:

REASON FOR REFERRAL:

EXAMINATIONS:

stock makes your report readily identifiable in a chart, case file, or school folder and is, at the same time, good public relations. Each time a folder containing one of your reports is opened, the color will stand out and your name will come to mind!

While it is not the purpose of this book to tell you how to write a consultation report, there are some brief, basic facts of professional life of which you should be aware. For example, many psychologists write consultation reports that seem to be written either for other psychologists or for the personal edification of the report writer. That is, they often tend to be wordy, overly long, and filled with highly technical terms that have little or no meaning for the person reading the report.

In private practice it is essential that consultation reports be written for the person (or agency) for whom they are intended. These reports should be clear, simple in language, directed to the questions posed, and *brief*. When a report is overly long, the tendency is to quickly turn to the summary, if there is one, and read only that. When the language is too technical and obscure (or esoteric), the tendency is to skim or disregard it altogether. (Harry Stack Sullivan once said, in writing about mental health professionals, that we speak a language that is so esoteric that we cannot communicate with anyone outside of the profession and we only have the illusion of communicating with each other.) In the final analysis, when the report is too long or too technical, the tendency is to find another consultant who will write reports that can be quickly and easily understood. You must always keep the reader of the report in mind—thus, reports on the same child should be different when prepared for a school or a physician in general practice or an attorney. Their needs for the case are different, which should be reflected by the reports.

Sooner or later you will begin to receive referrals from physicians and other professionals who have heard about you or met you. Very often these referrals will come in the form of a telephone call from the patient, who merely says that it has been suggested by Dr. Smith that he/she call you. Such patients may even be vague regarding the reasons for referral. At such times it is a good idea to call the source of referral for clarification of the reason for the referral and the services expected from you. There may, for example, be a patient referred by a general practitioner because the physician just doesn't have the time to sit with a patient who has no specific physical complaint but who needs the chance to ventilate feelings and get emotional support. At other times the referral may have been made because the referring professional has a vague idea that there is "something emotional going on," and wants you to find out what it may be! In other words, you also have the responsibility of helping professionals make appropriate referrals and ask the appropriate questions of you. They will usually be delighted that you recognize that they are unskilled in "shrink talk" and will be gratified that you are willing to take the time to instruct them in this foreign language.

All of the foregoing has used the referring physician as the example. In fact, the same is true of the attorney, the educator, the clergyman, and almost anyone who may refer cases to you. Thus, clarity of communication—in both directions—is an important key to good relationships with sources of referral. And, in the long run, there is better service to the patient when such clear communication exists.

It can often be helpful to visit an agency that uses your services as a resource in order to clarify for yourself what their needs are and how you can best help them in terms of report writing and communication in general. School personnel, for example, will be glad to talk with you, show you classes in operation, and discuss their needs in terms of the services you can provide. You, in turn, may discover new and innovative ways in which you can provide professional services to them.

When you are seeing a treatment patient who has been referred, it is a good idea to keep the referring professional posted on the general progress of the case. This doesn't have to be especially frequent, nor does it have to be very formal. A telephone call every few months or a brief note from time to time lets the other professional know that the patient is still being seen, that you are meeting your responsibility to communicate with the referral source, and that you want to maintain contact.

At the conclusion of therapy it is always a good idea to send a treatment summary—for failures as well as for successes. In this way the referring professional is aware of the final disposition of the case and, in the instance of the unsuccessful case, is made aware that you, too, are human!

Most important, perhaps, is the general rule to never turn away a referral if at all possible. Many successful practitioners leave open time in their schedule for consultations. If you have a full schedule and simply have no room for any more therapy cases, for example, it is still a good plan to see patients for at least one or two interviews in order to screen them and then, perhaps, refer them to a colleague for treatment. This is a valuable service and should not be underestimated. As indicated earlier, many times the referral source only knows that the patient "may have problems," and you can be helpful in determining the nature of these difficulties and suggesting a colleague who may be the most appropriate person to manage the case. Further, when you refuse cases because of a full schedule, you run the risk of losing that referral source. As indicated at the beginning of this chapter, no source of referral should be considered permanent. If you are too busy to see someone's cases, he will look for a psychologist who *can* see them. And don't worry about those hours in the week when no consultations are scheduled. The time can be used for professional reading or some other activity that pleases you and helps you to relax.

If you do see patients in consultation, it is a good idea to conduct follow-up of your own. A call to the referring professional some weeks or months after your report has been received will often yield information that will help you sharpen your own evaluative skills in future, similar cases. Again, this helps in building the relationship with those who send you cases and demonstrates to them that you are, indeed, interested in them and the patients that they have sent to you.

Attorneys are increasingly utilizing the services of psychologists as consultants. The average clinician in either a "general practice" or a specialty will be consulted about child custody cases, marital and divorce problems, and questions concerning organic brain damage arising from varying kinds of accidents. Some of these cases have to do with the decision-making process of the judge or jury in terms of custody of children, for example. Others have to do with monies based upon lawsuits arising out of accidents. In all these cases, you are being consulted in your professional capacity—as an "expert." It is extremely important to be completely aware of the facts of the case both in terms of what, precisely, is expected of you and in terms of the specific details of the matter at hand. The attorney will provide you with all the information you request (and frequently more than you have asked for). In such cases the psychologist must be extremely clear in his own mind as to whether or not he can, in fact, respond to the request of the attorney and, at the same time, call his shots as he sees them. The attorney may, in the long run, be just as grateful to you if you give him a report that is not necessarily helpful to his client's case, since it will help him to prepare for what the other side may present from *their* expert witness.

If a psychologist becomes "too obliging" to referring attorneys, he may become known in the legal community as a member of the oldest profession. This is not to say that one can't make a fine living by being extra obliging to referring attorneys. However, one must, at the same time, make decisions and personal judgments concerning individual morality, ethics, and overall theoretical orientation to consultations. My own view is that none of these should ever be negotiable.

In writing reports for lawyers it is usually advisable to use technical terminology along with a clear explanation. A typical passage in a report might read, "The patient showed difficulties with fine motor coordination. That is, while easily able to climb stairs and ride a bicycle (gross motor coordination), she was unable to adequately handle a pencil, had great difficulty in copying geometric figures accurately, and could not pick up a small pellet with thumb and forefinger." Thus, you are providing the lawyer with the technical terminology that he needs for potential examination or cross-examination while, at the same time, you are clearly defining what you mean.

If you provide consultation services for attorneys you must also be prepared to appear in court as an "expert witness" from time to time. While you will be reimbursed for the time you spend, it can be a difficult experience.

Finally, in your consulting for the legal profession, do not accept contingency fee arrangements—a fee based upon the financial settlement of the case. If you do this you are automatically involved in the case in a non-objective way, since collection of your fee is dependent upon the patient's winning. Not only may this serve to limit objectivity, but it is also a serious breach of ethical practice.

Clergymen will very frequently refer patients. There are increasing numbers of clergymen, of all denominations, who have been professionally trained in pastoral counseling, and they can, as a result, fairly quickly identify those individuals who need the services of a mental health professional with training and skills beyond their own. The cases referred by clergymen ordinarily run the same gamut as those referred by other professionals, except clergymen refer fewer people with marital problems. This is usually an area of specific training for the trained pastoral counselor.

Personal, ongoing contact with local clergy can help stimulate and maintain regular referrals. Clergy will often want to know about your own religious identification and feelings. They are not necessarily seeking referral sources that match their own sense of religious identification but, rather, are trying to understand what manner of patients they feel they can or cannot send to you. This is a perfectly legitimate expectation on their part and, as a result, candor on your part will be recognized and appreciated by them.

As your practice develops you will begin to receive increasing numbers of referrals from GP's (Grateful Patients). In fact, many senior practitioners find that the largest part of their practice is made up of people who have been referred by former patients. If the referral is made by a patient you are currently seeing, it is usually best to make no mention during your contact with the "old patient" of the fact that the person he or she has referred is being seen. This is consistent with the needs of confidentiality and will, in the long run, be appreciated by the old patient. Besides, if the patient has made a referral, he has probably already discussed the first visit with the person he has referred. If, on the other hand, you are asked whether the friend or family member has, indeed, come in, it is appropriate to respond in the affirmative and say "Thanks" for the referral, without any further comment.

During the course of a therapeutic relationship there will be many times when a patient will deal with issues that require the services of a professional of another discipline. For example, many patients need legal services or specialized medical services. This provides the practitioner with an opportunity to both be of assistance to the patient and, at the same time, cement good relationships with referral sources. It is both ethical and appropriate to refer such patients to those professionals who have been making referrals to you. When you do this, it may be via a note sent along with the patient, by a phone call, or by suggesting to the patient that he or she tell the other professional that you have suggested that he or she call. Here, too, a follow-up call from you is indicated. The professional to whom you have made the referral may have some questions about the case and, at the same time, the call will serve as a reminder that you are making referrals. Calling is suggested because it is never safe to assume that other professionals will necessarily follow the rules set down in this chapter and call you!

Finally, there is the overall question of gifts and entertainment of sources of referral. The regulations of the Internal Revenue Services are in a state of constant change—or so it seems. Thus it is not safe to assume that a gift to a referral source at holiday time or an invitation to luncheon or your home is necessarily a business expense and, hence, a tax deductible item. Your accountant will be able to advise you as to this aspect of your practice.

At any rate, it is appropriate to send gifts and entertain those who make referrals to you. If someone has, for example, sent you a number of cases over the course of a year, a gift at holiday time is one way of expressing your thanks. Taking people to dinner or lunch or entertaining them at your home is yet another way of expressing gratitude. Entertaining your source of referral is also an opportunity for you to get to know each other in a new, more personal way. The significant factor, then, is not whether such activity is tax deductible as a business expense. The issue is that these activities can be practice-enhancing. However, it is important to remember, "Moderation in all things." Too much gift-giving or entertaining could smack of a special kind of bribery, while insufficient recognition or appreciation could communicate to your referral sources that you don't care or that you don't need them.

8
Fees: Setting Them, Collecting Them

The determination and collection of fees may well be the most anxiety-provoking issue of private practice. Fees are not ordinarily discussed as part of the practitioner's training and, as professionals, we are presumed to be above such crass matters. Thus, a mystique has arisen about the private practitioner which serves only to further confuse the beginner and to heighten anxiety.

The full-time practitioner depends entirely upon fees for sustenance. This fact alone is one of the deterrents that keeps many people away from full-time practice—the anxious feeling of, "How can I support myself (and my family) without an assured income?" There is nothing mysterious about fees and their collection. This chapter will attempt to clarify and bring some sense to the issue.

Fees are not the same in all areas. Ordinarily, the large metropolitan areas have a somewhat higher fee structure than the less densely populated areas. There is a kind of logic to this. Big cities are more expensive to live in than are small towns and, hence, incomes must be higher. An apartment and a loaf of bread—and a session with a psychologist—

cost more in New York City than they do in Saddlesore, Texas.

There is usually a range of fees charged by practitioners in any given area, which is based upon "seniority" in the profession in terms of years of experience and, concomitantly, how well-known the practitioner may be. The range is usually not very wide, with the spread being about five to ten dollars per visit.

The best way to find out the general fee structure in your community is, simply, to ask colleagues who are already in practice. If you are the first to practice in your community, then feel free to ask colleagues in similar, nearby communities. Most will be glad to give you this information.

The first cautionary note is: Don't sell yourself short! If you have the self-esteem to feel that you are ready to go into practice, then you are worth what the going rate is for your area. If you charge a fee that is less than others, you may be communicating the idea that you are not really worth the usual fees—and then, you may be correct.

The fee should be discussed frankly and openly with your patients in the very first session. Unless the patient raises the issue early in the first meeting, it is usually best to reserve the closing few minutes for the talk about fees. By that time the patient will have had a chance to assess you and will have already reached some conclusion as to whether or not to continue seeing you. Thus, you have established a beginning relationship and talk of money will not be quite so difficult for either the patient or you. At that point you should indicate what your fee is and how you wish to be paid.

Some professionals require the patient to pay the fee each time they come. Others are content to send a monthly bill, indicating that it must be paid within that month. Still others give the patient the option of choosing either method of payment, feeling that mode of payment should be within the confines of the patient's reality situation. Whichever of these modalities of payment you select, it is important that it be quite clearly stated to the patient and that there be no ambiguity.

The current inflationary trend has resulted in escalating office expenses over the past few years. This has been reflected in increased bills for heat, light, office supplies, etc. The personal expenses of the practitioner have also increased sharply (as they have for everyone). As a result, it sometimes becomes necessary to increase fees to meet these expenses. There are two general ways of handling this in your practice. Some professionals increase the fee for everyone they are currently seeing, as well as for those new patients who arrive in the office. Other professionals determine what their new fee will have to be and charge this only to new arrivals, feeling that they have an implicit contract with "old" patients and cannot change the fee in midstream. If you decide to charge the new fee for everyone, it is best to send a letter to each of your current patients advising them of the new fee, along with some explanatory information. In addition, it is best to invite them to discuss it with you the next time you meet.

There are many other fee arrangements that are often made by professionals in private practice. One of these is the "sliding fee schedule." In this case the private practitioner functions much like a community clinic. An evaluation is made of the patient's income and financial responsibilities, which may entail some substantiation of the patient's resources such as paycheck stubs, last year's income tax form, mortgage payment receipts, etc. A fee is then established which is deemed appropriate based upon these realities. With this kind of fee-setting procedure, it is important for each patient to know that this is the procedure with all who come to the office and that the fees that other patients pay may be different from what he or she is paying.

With this approach to fees it may also be necessary to re-evaluate patients' financial status from time to time when their fortunes either improve or decline and, hence, a new fee is appropriate. You must also be prepared to be taken advantage of, on occasion, when a patient will not be entirely truthful about financial status. However, this possibility does not necessarily mean that the sliding fee schedule is not a good idea, for with such a strucutre there are, indeed, people who can avail themselves of your services who might not otherwise be able to do so. This is especially true for those communities where there are few, if any, mental health services available.

Still another method of fee payment might be called the "deferred payment plan." With this method of payment the patient is charged the regular, standard fee for services, but is permitted to pay a lesser amount each month against the fee. The balance of the fee that remains unpaid accrues until the relationship is terminated, and the patient continues to pay the predetermined monthly sum until full payment has been made. With this plan the patient can feel that he is not a "charity case," and the psychologist feels a sense of adequate reimbursement for services performed. Like the sliding fee schedule, this method will also involve an evaluation of the patient's financial status. An added advantage of this method of payment, for the practitioner, is that the monthly payments, after termination, provide a "cushion" during the lean months of vacation time. When patients (and the psychologist) go away and income is sharply curtailed, those paying on the deferred plan provide a baseline of income.

No matter what fee you set and no matter what method of payment you determine, the fee must be mutually and fully understood by both you and your patient. As long as there is complete understanding of the financial arrangements and mutual responsibilities, these will not interfere with the patient/psychologist relationship.

Patients sometimes miss appointments, and your policy about paying for missed appointments should be clear to them and to you. Some professionals simply accept this as one of the hazards of practice and do not make an issue of it. Others require payment for missed appointments regardless of the reason or how far in advance notice is given. Still others have a "24-hour" policy—if notice of a missed appointment is given 24 hours in advance, there is no fee charged. If either of the latter two is to be your method, it is important that your patients be aware of this at the beginning of treatment. One way of reinforcing the existence of the 24-hour rule is to use appointment cards as illustrated in Figure 9.

FIGURE 9

M_____

HAS AN APPOINTMENT WITH

ALVIN M. JONES, PH.D.
965 WALT WHITMAN ROAD
MELVILLE, N. Y. 11746
—
TELEPHONE 421-1200

FOR

MON. _____AT _____

TUES. _____AT _____

WED. _____AT _____

THURS. _____AT _____

FRI. _____AT _____

SAT. _____AT _____

IF UNABLE TO KEEP THIS APPOINT-
MENT KINDLY GIVE 24 HOURS
NOTICE .OTHERWISE CHARGE WILL
BE MADE FOR TIME RESERVED.

There are some practitioners who draw up a mutually agreed upon "contract" which outlines the responsibilities of each party and is signed by both. The psychologist and patient then each have a copy.

If you do group therapy there is usually a lower hourly fee set, per person, than there is for individual therapy. The size of this fee varies from area to area (as with individual fees) and also varies according to the seniority and reputation of the practitioner. Again, consultation with colleagues can be helpful and instructive.

Even in the best-run practice, patient bills sometimes have a way of building up to the point where payment may become unmanageable for the patient and unacceptably delayed for the practitioner. Hence, you should develop a rule-of-thumb as to how large a bill can be before it becomes impossible for the patient and hostility-provoking for you. At (or preferably before) that point you must take a firm stand and deal with the issue directly. There are a variety of appropriate methods, some of which are: termination of the relationship; downward revision of the regular fee, thus permitting "catching up"; or a temporary hiatus of the relationship until a significant part of the bill has been paid. There may also be times when you find yourself heavily invested in a case and are willing to simply accept the loss. While this is admittedly not good business practice, we are (I hope) in the profession because we care about people.

Some practitioners are beginning to use credit cards for fee collection. One can make arrangements with organizations like American Express, Diners Club, VISA, etc. If you do this, you will have to fill out forms, use the little machine to imprint the form, and file your own copies with the credit card company at regular intervals. The credit card companies receive a percentage of your fee (usually between two and five percent), but it does mean assured payment for you.

The services of psychologists are now covered by major medical insurance policies in more states than ever before. CHAMPUS (Civilian Health and Medical Plan for the Uniformed Forces) also covers psychological treatment, as does Federal Employees Blue Cross/Blue Shield. Patients on Medicaid are also covered for psychological services. As a result, the services of the psychologist are realistically available to more people than previously. There is, however, a new and increasing burden on the psychologist in terms of completing forms and reading insurance manuals in order to properly complete those forms. Payment from insurance companies and CHAMPUS can ordinarily be in one of two ways—you can either be directly reimbursed by the insurance carrier for that part of your fee for which they are responsible, or the patient can pay your full fee and then be reimbursed by the carrier for that part for which the patient is covered. If you choose to be reimbursed by the company yourself, it is important that the patient sign that part of the insurance form which indicates "Assignment of Benefits." The method you choose is largely a matter of choice. If you wish the patient to pay in full and be reimbursed by the company, you may experience long delays in payment, but the responsibility for who shall pay you is clear. If, on the other hand, you choose the "Assignment of Benefits" route, you have the bird-in-the-hand of ultimate payment for at least partial payment by the insurance carrier.

Medicaid pays you a flat fee, regardless of what your regular fee may be. With Medicaid it is necessary that you carefully read the manual provided by the insurance carrier in your state so that you are aware of all of the requirements for proper completion of forms. Also, Medicaid requires special authorization by a state agency after the first $300 of payments, which will require still more forms to be sent.

Familiarity with the manual is of critical importance if you wish to be paid.

If your state is one that has a clearly defined law that provides for psychologists' services to be included in any policy that indicates coverage for outpatient services by psychiatrists, you will have few difficulties with insurance companies. But it is a good idea to keep a few photocopies of the law in your file cabinet. Insurance companies sometimes maintain that they are not aware of the law in your state and sending them a copy of the law will often clear up the problem.

More and more insurance companies are using the National Register of Health Service Providers in Psychology as a basis for payment of benefits. It is, then, a good idea to make application and have your name included in the Register.

If you choose to send monthly bills, it is a good idea to use a fairly standard professional billhead, as in Figure 10. You will note that this bill is itemized for dates seen as well as services performed and the fees. Most patients appreciate receiving an itemization, which they can check against their personal records. Also, most insurance companies require that the policy holder include itemized bills along with the form that you will send in.

There will be patients who simply don't pay their bills. For those who are seen on a regular basis in therapy this is, of course, a therapeutic issue as well as a fiscal matter and can usually be dealt with in sessions with the patient. However, there will be a few who don't pay and drop out of treatment after running up a bill. There are others who are seen in consultation for one or more visits and don't pay their bill.

What can you do to collect from these individuals? Well, there are some techniques that have proven effective for many practitioners. One method is to write a letter, detailing the patient's financial responsibility to you and indicating that you anticipate payment. It is usually a good idea to invite the

FIGURE 10

STATEMENT

TELEPHONE 421-1200

ALVIN MYLES JONES, PH.D.
965 WALT WHITMAN ROAD
MELVILLE, N. Y. 11746

_____ 1 October ₁₉ 78

Mr. John C. Kidd

10 Pleasant Lane

Somewhere, New Jersey

FOR PROFESSIONAL SERVICES:

9/7/78	Parent interview	50.00
9/11,13,18	Examinations; James	150.00
9/25	Parent interpretive conf.	50.00
		250.00

patient to call and discuss some realistic method of regular, partial payments. This will often produce positive results. A second method is to use collection stickers, serially, as in Figure 11, for three consecutive months. These are available from most commercial stationers.

FIGURE 11

YOUR attention is respectfully called to this account which, no doubt, has been overlooked. An early settlement of same will be greatly appreciated.   SG-1

PLEASE give this account your immediate attention. It is long past due and settlement must be made without further delay.   SG-2

EVERY courtesy has been extended you regarding the payment of this long over due account. Unless paid at once it will be placed in the usual channels for collection provided by law.   3

FIGURE 12

> ### FINAL NOTICE
>
> *If this account is not paid on or before*
>
> ....
>
> *Papers may be filed with the Clerk of the District Court which starts immediate Legal proceedings under the New Jersey Law. Accounts up to $500.00 can be collected without Constable, Sheriff or Attorney fee. All costs must be paid by Debtor.*   ©

If these do not produce payment it may be necessary to afix a final sticker to a bill which indicates your rights under the small claims court procedures in your state (see Figure 12). This, too, will usually be effective. Following these techniques there are a series of form letters available from many stationers which purport to come from a mythical collection service. While they may be helpful, there is a flavor of mendacity to their use and you may, as a result, have some objection to utilizing them.

If all of these methods fail you still have some choices. You can engage a professional collection agency and refer your delinquent accounts to them. They will then pursue the matter with a great deal of vigor and, much of the time, will make the collection for you. Their ordinary fee is fifty percent of whatever they collect. (Exorbitant as this may seem, fifty percent of *something* is better than fifty percent of nothing.) A possible drawback to the use of a collection agency is that they often pursue small acounts with somewhat less vigor than they do larger ones. Further, they sometimes have to refer the matter to an attorney, which may mean a smaller eventual return for you.

Another method is to retain an attorney to collect for you. The attorney, like the collection agency, will pursue the matter with vigor. However, attorneys are frequently loathe to accept for collection a bill they feel is too small to warrant the amount of work they may have to put in on it, since their fee is usually about the same as the collection agency. On the other hand, the attorney is prepared to go to court to collect, if necessary, even though the fee remains the same.

Finally, in most states you have recourse to small claims court. The maximum amount of money involved varies from state to state, but it is a method that will usually produce results and you will collect the entire fee yourself. However, you must make the decision as to whether or not you want to go this route. It involves going to the clerk of the court and filing a claim, for which there is a fee. You must usually also pay the fee for the marshal to serve a summons on the recalcitrant patient, and then you will have to appear in court for the hearing. If you win the case, all of your court costs will be awarded to you (i.e., the patient will have to pay them). But you may also have to pay a marshal to go out and collect for you. Most practitioners avoid this method because it is so time-consuming.

In fact, most psychologists report a collection rate of 90 percent or better. You can too, if you take all of the precautions outlined at the beginning of this chapter. A patient who is informed and who has participated in the decision-making as to the mode of payment is ordinarily one who will pay.

Nevertheless, there will always be some fees that will go uncollected. These uncollected fees are *not* deductible items for income tax purposes. They are not considered bad debts, and, since we deal in services rather than products, there is no way to recoup the losses via a "tax break." Thus, it behooves the practitioner to have a clear, functioning system of fees and fee collection.

Finally, it is probable that your expenses, at the beginning of your practice, will exceed income. Hang in! And try not to fall into the trap of taking patients that you would ordinarily feel were inappropriate for your practice only because your fiscal situation is tight. This is, of course, unethical and may damage your reputation and, ultimately, your practice.

9

Planning Ahead —
Way Ahead

Those of us committed to a full-time, long-term career as professional, privately practicing psychologists must be prepared to plan for our own financial future, as well as that of our families. In private practice there are no state pension plans, there is no accrued sick leave (with pay), and there is no paid vacation. Consequently, the planning and preparation for all of these matters are left to us to do on our own. In fact, many professionals attempt to plan for these matters quite literally on their own, despite the painful truth that most of us are ill equipped for such a major task.

Fortunately, though, there are various key people in the community who are trained to assist and guide the practicing professional through the uncharted seas (for us, not them) of life and health insurance, long-term financial planning, retirement planning, and the daily fiscal operation of the practice. Ordinarily, one thinks of the banker, the attorney, the accountant, the insurance agent, and the investment counselor when making such plans. These fiscal/planning experts can be consulted individually but, more often, the best consultants prefer to work in concert when matters arise that affect their mutual areas of expertise. That is, your insurance man or your banker may well prefer to work in tandem with your accountant or your attorney. Or your attorney, for example, may suggest meeting with your accountant and your investment counselor. This is all to your benefit.

You will need, all through the life of your practice, professionals in all of the above areas. We often talk of "shoppers" —those who go from professional to professional until they find one who appears to meet their needs. While those of us in the mental health professions sometimes tend to disparage this kind of behavior, it is, in fact, a fine idea when seeking out experts to help us. The truth is that mental health professionals are as easily cowed by financial or legal experts as patients who shop around are by us. Since our financial security depends on the expertise of these individuals, we should shop around until we find those who appear to understand our needs, our profession, and us.

LAWYERS

Your prospective attorney should not only be expert in the area of contracts, but should also have a good understanding of the fiscal needs and problems of a private practice, be aware of the current status of legislation and rulings covering issues like confidentiality, and be prepared to deal with all of the myriad questions that a private practitioner might be asking him anywhere along the line.

The attorney is your resource person for any contract into which you may enter. He should, for example, review any leases or any contracts for purchase of materials or services before you sign. Since most such documents, as we know, are almost totally incomprehensible to anyone not legally trained, using an attorney can save many possible headaches. One practitioner, for example, thought he was leasing some dictating equipment with an option to buy it very inexpensively at the end of the leasing period. When the leasing period was up, he discovered, to his chagrin, that the cost was so much greater than he had been told that it was just not worth his while to pick up the option to purchase. A lawyer could have reviewed the original contract and advised him to either have the terms changed or not sign.

The attorney can also be an invaluable resource in some of the professional aspects of your practice. For example, a child may be referred to you because of emotional difficulties. Upon interview with the mother you discover that the parents are separated. Early in your relationship with the child you receive a letter from the estranged husband (who is totally supporting the family) ordering you to stop seeing the child. His rationale is that since he is paying support, he has control over what happens to the child and what professionals the child may see. Your attorney can advise you as to whether or not he has the right to do this or, on the other hand, whether the parent with whom the child lives has the ultimate control.

Thus, the selection of your attorney can be crucial in the long view of your practice. Shop until you find one who appears to meet your criteria and is personally compatible. That is, he should be someone to whom you can relate easily without his causing you to feel deprecated because you don't have his professional knowledge and expertise. (Sound familiar? I thought so.)

ACCOUNTANTS

Your accountant, too, can be a pivotal person. He should be prepared to answer all of your questions and meet all of your accounting needs promptly and efficiently. The accountant, ideally, should be someone who has had other professional people as clients and, best of all, other psychologists. If you find someone whom you like and trust, but who hasn't had this kind of experience, then you should acquaint him as much as possible with the nature of your practice and your financial life-style. If you want to kid yourself, your wife, or your colleagues about your financial status, that's okay (I guess). But never, never try to kid your accountant. Anything less than complete honesty with him could mean ultimate financial disaster for you.

The accountant will set up your bookkeeping system for you so that accurate records can be kept and he can keep tabs on your financial affairs. He will be able to tell you, at regular intervals during the year, just what the financial state of your practice may be. He can advise you as to what kind of major expenditures to make, and when. You will be advised as to what expenditures may or may not be tax deductible as business expenses. The accountant will, of course, prepare your Federal and State income tax forms for you. He will be able to tell you how much estimated taxes you will have to pay each quarter and will prepare the forms that must accompany each payment. This is important since private practitioners must pay their income tax in advance, based upon estimated income for the year ahead. If, by the end of the year, you have estimated wrongly and come up more than 20 percent short, there is also a penalty to pay!

In other words, your accountant should be much more than the person who prepares your income tax forms once a year. He should be your constant advisor in terms of the direction you take in the management of your money.

BANKERS

As long as you are in practice, and as long as you see you and your practice (for the sake of simplicity we will henceforth refer to the dual "you and your practice" merely as "you") as being a viable, growing entity, you will need a banker. Note that I did not say "bank"—I said *"banker."* Banks, these days, are quite literally a dime a dozen. You can't throw a stone without hitting a new or branch bank that is being built. This is to your advantage, because all of these banks are looking for business and you are just the kind of business they are looking for. You represent to them a trained, stable, mature professional person who will funnel large sums of money through their banking institution during all the years that you will be in practice. You represent the safest kind of loan money to them—safer, for example, than the small merchant who may actually gross far more dollars per year than you do.

Money is a commodity that is bought and sold, and the person (bank) giving the best service and the best price (terms) makes the sale. As a result, banks are ready to court you because they want your business. When you are ready to open your office and need money and financial advice, you should first shop around for a banker. Your banker, to begin with, should be someone fairly high in the bank's hierarchy. One good way to begin is to call a local banking institution and make an appointment to meet with the president. Tell him of your plans and needs and also that you are looking for a banker with whom you can work during the years ahead. You should also let him know that you are comparison shopping. After he has either decided to work with you himself or referred you to an appropriate officer of the bank, you can then get into the details of your own immediate needs. A competent banker will be able to both respond to your current requirements and indicate to you the other services that his bank will be able to offer you over the years ahead (mortgage monies, loans for capital improvements, etc.).

Now repeat this performance of yours with two or three

other banks/bankers. You will find that, by and large, they will vary as to the terms they can offer, arrangements they are willing to make, and the personality of the banker with whom you will be dealing. Your banker can be a key person in terms of the way you use your money now and prepare for the future.

INSURANCE MEN

Your insurance man should be able to tell you what special kinds of coverage you may need for your office furnishings and for your valuable collection of professional books. You will be advised as to what kind of liability insurance you may need for employees. Do you, for example, need insurance coverage for the cleaning person who comes in once a week; also what kind of coverage is needed for the part-time secretary? Must you also have workman's compensation coverage? And what kind? Do you need a liability policy in case a patient slips and breaks a leg on the old carpeting that you have been planning to replace? Should you take out income protection insurance from him or is the APA plan a better one? (The competent insurance person, who sees you as the long-term client that you could be, will be quite honest about this kind of issue. It's good business.) You will also be advised, usually at yearly intervals, regarding the appreciation in value of your building and possessions and, as a result, the need for increased insurance coverage.

Your insurance man can not only advise you as to the coverage you need for all of these areas but also advise you about ways to secure the future of your family now or for the years ahead. The capable insurance man can provide you, for example, with varying kinds of life insurance coverage that will assure your family of a life-style that you would want them to have should you die. Also, depending upon the kind of company and agent you deal with, he can also help you with fiscal planning in terms of combinations of insurance and investments that will make your own declining years comfortable.

Professional liability insurance is available from an agency that has the "franchise" from the American Psychological Association, at fees which are remarkably low compared with premiums paid by many medical practitioners. Also, there are other insurance carriers who write such policies. If you don't want the APA insurance coverage, or if you'd like to do some comparison shopping, your own insurance broker can make inquiries for you and then, as with other coverage, advise you as to the best course for you to take.

In choosing an insurance agent you must, once again, shop, look and listen. You should interview both independent agents (those who are self-employed and represent more than one insurance company) and those who work for one company as an employee and are on a commission basis. You should look into stock companies (where you are a customer/client) and mutual companies (where you are, in effect, one of the owners). You should have the representatives of each kind of company carefully explain the difference. (Each will also, of course, explain why his company and his plan are the best.)

STOCK BROKERS

Finally, there are the people who sell stock, bonds, and all the ramifications of these in terms of mutual funds, stock investment programs, etc. Here, again, shopping is extremely important. Do you, for example, want a small firm with few employees where one of them will give you a great deal of attention and get to know you? Or do you want a large firm where the person you deal with is a specialist in setting up investment programs for professionals? Do you want to invest your savings in stocks? Municipal bonds? Blue chips? Blue sky? Or what? The right person can advise you and set up an appropriate program based upon your long- and short-term needs.

We have been talking about professionals in areas that are far afield from our own. They, too, tend to talk in a language that is often highly technical, extremely obscure/confusing (to us), and filled with terms that we scarcely understand. How, then, can we effectively communicate with them when there is no really basic technical language that we can share? Simple: Don't be afraid to confess your ignorance. On the contrary, use your ignorance of the legal tongue, or the investment language, or accountancy patois, as a weapon. When your consultant-to-be says something you don't understand, tell him immediately. When your banker begins talking in terms that make you feel faint, ask for verbal smelling salts. Insist on words of one syllable and be frank in telling them that you are a fiscal (or accounting, or legal, or etc.) idiot. If they still won't explicate in terms that you can really understand—flee, for you have made a mistake and gone to the wrong person. However, most of the time competent professionals will be glad to talk in a common language, once you have made it clear that you don't understand theirs.

SELLING THE PRACTICE

Perhaps one of the greatest investments of all, for your post-practice future, is the practice itself. Increasingly, as more and more psychologists enter practice, there exists the real opportunity to sell your practice when you are ready for retirement.

The sale of an independent practice is very much like the sale of any commodity with, of course, some obvious differences. The similarities are those concerned with volume (cash flow), furnishings and equipment, and "good will" (your reputation in the community). The difference is the fact that your practice deals with people, and you may not be able to transfer all of your caseload to the psychologist who purchases your practice. However, this, in the long run, is a minor matter if the sale and transfer of the practice are handled adequately.

Selling price of a practice is usually derived from the annual gross income; the exact figure is ordinarily arrived at by averaging the gross of the few years prior to the sale. Payment, of course, may be made in a lump sum (usually unrealistic and unlikely) or, more frequently, over a period of years. This, of course, both assures you of a regular supplement to your other retirement income for a few years and, at the same time, cuts down on the tax bite that would take place with a one-time payment.

After a buyer has been found for the practice the process usually goes through various stages. The new practitioner in your office is ordinarily announced as an associate of yours, which gives him a chance to be introduced to the community and identified as being "with" you. During this period of time you may transfer newly referred cases to him while you wind down with your own current caseload. Following this stage you may begin to cut down on your own hours in the office, turning over more and more responsibility to the new "owner."

The third phase might be one where you are now identified as a consultant to the practice, seeing an occasional consultation or doing an occasional preliminary interview. Finally, you bow out altogether, retiring to your boat or special spot on the beach. The entire process, to be handled appropriately with maximum benefits to patients, the new owner, and yourself, should take at least one year. At the end of that time the new owner of the practice should have established his own identity, while you have gradually eased your way out gracefully, comfortably, and ethically.

It goes without saying that *all* of the details of the sale and transfer of the practice should be handled with the help and consultation of your attorney, accountant, and, possibly, investment counselor. In this way you will be able to realize, and enjoy, the most of your selling price.

Do not underestimate the ultimate cash value of your practice. The better the job you do in the years ahead, the greater the likelihood that you will have nurtured a highly desirable "product" when you are ready to retire.

Index

"ABC" practice technique, 17
"ABPP," 43
Accountants:
    audits of, 53
    functions of, general, 93-94, 100
    and incorporation, 16
Account cards, 52-53
Accounting procedures, 12, 55, 58
Adolescents:
    transportation problems of, 19-20
    treatment of, as specialty, 14
    waiting room needs of, 29
American Express cards, 83
American Psychological Association
    (APA):
    ethical standards of, 10
    insurance coverage, group, 8, 96, 97
Announcements, office opening, 63
Answering machines, electronic, 39-41
Answering services, 38-39
Appointment books, 53-54
Appointment cards, 51, 82
Aquinas, St. Thomas, xi
Associative partnerships, 10. See also
    Partnership practices
Attorneys:
    for building purchase, 26
    communications with, 74-75
    for contracts, 92-93
    and fee collection, 89
    functions of, general, 92-93, 100
    for leases, 24, 92-93
    for partnership formation, 11-12
    and referrals, 71, 72, 74
Authorization/permission forms, 54-
    56, 58

Bankers, functions of, 94-96
Bathrooms. See Toilet facilities
Behavior modification therapy, 14
Billheads, 49, 50. See also Stationery
Bookkeeping, in partnership, 12. See
    also Accounting procedures
Brain damage, organic, 74

Call forwarding, 41-42. See also Tele-
    phones
Capitalization, 60-61. See also Office
    establishment
Cerebral palsy clinics, 64
Certification, 4. See also Licensure
CHAMPUS (Civilian Health and
    Medical Plan for the Uni-
    formed Forces), 84
Checking account, 55
Children:
    custody cases, 74
    treatment of, as specialty, 14
    waiting room needs of, 29, 30-31
Classified ads, for offices, 27
Cleaning, office:
    economy in, false, 59-60
    in partnerships, 10
    services for, 60
Clergymen, referrals from, 75-76
Collection agencies, 88. See also Fees
Confidentiality, legal advice on, 92
Conjoint family therapy, 13. See also
    Family therapy
Consultations:
    and attorneys, 74-75
    forms for, 70
    and practice, sale of, 99-100

101